The NSC Staff

The NSC Staff

Counseling the Council

Christopher C. Shoemaker

Westview Press
BOULDER • SAN FRANCISCO • OXFORD

To Terri

Copyright © 1991 by Westview Press, Inc., except for the following material, which is in the public domain: portions of Chapters 1–3, previously published by the U.S. Army War College Strategic Studies Institute under the title *The Decisional Dilemma: Structure, Function, and the NSC Staff* (Washington, D.C.: U.S. Government Printing Office, 1990), and portions of Chapter 5, previously published in *Parameters* 19, no. 3 (September 1989), under the title "Rebuilding the Policy Crucible."

Published in 1991 in the United States of America by Westview Press, Inc., 5500 Central Avenue, Boulder, Colorado 80301, and in the United Kingdom by Westview Press, 36 Lonsdale Road, Summertown, Oxford OX2 7EW

Library of Congress Cataloging-in-Publication Data
Shoemaker, Christopher C.
  The NSC staff: counseling the council / Christopher Shoemaker.
    p. cm.
  Includes bibliographical references (p.   ) and index.
  ISBN 0-8133-7922-9. — ISBN 0-8133-7923-7 (if published as
  a paperback)
  1. National Security Council (U.S.).   2. United States—National
security.   I. Title.
UA23.15.S49   1991
353.0089—dc20   90-12508
                                                                      CIP

Printed and bound in the United States of America

The paper used in this publication meets the requirements of the American National Standard for Permanence of Paper for Printed Library Materials Z39.48-1984.

10   9   8   7   6   5   4   3   2   1

Contents

Foreword

The management of national security has long presented a governmental and organizational dilemma of the first order. As we look at the nature of the international environment, there is no cause to believe that this dilemma will become any less pronounced in the future. The demands of national security and the accelerating rate at which decisions must be made argue for the development and implementation of the most effective management system possible.

The U.S. constitutional framework provides remarkably little guidance to a president in constructing a system for making national security policy. In fact, each president must invent his own system. Some, like Franklin Roosevelt and John Kennedy, have used informal groups of trusted advisers; others, like Harry Truman and Gerald Ford, have delegated policy-making to the secretary of state; still others, like Dwight Eisenhower, Richard Nixon, and Jimmy Carter, have centralized policy-making procedures within the White House, with the National Security Council apparatus assuming a vital organizing and coordinating role. Problems, such as the Iran-Contra affair, have often developed when a president has failed to provide clear lines of authority for the policy-making process.

In this book, Christopher C. Shoemaker comes to grips with this daunting issue as few other authors have. His analysis and his prescriptions are based on a realistic assessment of the complexity of national security and of the inadequacy of past systems in dealing with the issues in a systematic fashion. Of special importance is the need to refine and articulate the role of the National Security Council Staff along the lines proposed in this book. The NSC Staff must again become the focal point of the national security structure, with the presidential imprimatur necessary to make the system effective.

This is a book of significant value to both students and practitioners of national security. Students will benefit by seeing the practical dimensions of the NSC, and those charged with the management of national security should consider seriously the structural recommendations. It is a rare combination of intellectual insight and practical utility and contributes in a substantial way to the study of decision-making at the highest levels.

Zbigniew Brzezinski

Introduction

On November 3, 1986, the Beirut newsmagazine *Al Shiraa* reported that the United States had been secretly selling weapons to Iran, notwithstanding a formal arms embargo that had been in effect since the Tehran embassy seizure seven years before. This story was the tip of a policy and procedural iceberg that, when fully surfaced, would precipitate a major crisis for the Reagan administration. As the details of the issue were gradually revealed, it became apparent that, apart from raising serious questions of judgment, the Iran-Contra affair demonstrated some major problems within the National Security Council Staff, problems that called into question the very nature and function of that organization. For the first time in its often controversial history, the NSC Staff was subjected to serious public scrutiny, and calls for major reform arose from many quarters. Even those favorably disposed toward the administration began to ask how one small staff could wield so much power, even in the face of what was apparently determined opposition from the Department of State and the Department of Defense. For students and practitioners of national security policy, the fundamental procedural and structural questions posed in the wake of the Iran-Contra affair warrant serious attention.

Since its inception in 1947, the National Security Council Staff has assumed an increasingly significant role in the formulation of national security policy in the United States. What began as essentially an administrative and clerical support group for the National Security Council has evolved into what, without exaggeration, has become the single most powerful staff in Washington, eclipsing other departmental staffs which, by statute and custom, should have been dominant in their respective fields. This rise in power has been most often ascribed to the powerful personalities who have headed the NSC Staff. However, personalities, even those as strong as Zbigniew Brzezinski and Henry Kissinger, do not alone explain the remarkable bureaucratic clout of the NSC Staff. Indeed, during the Iran-Contra affair, the NSC Staff was headed by persons not noted for personal flair.

In order to understand the sources and implications of NSC Staff power, it is necessary to look beyond personalities and examine the functional roles played by the Staff as an institution. Only then does it become apparent that, regardless of the strengths or weaknesses of the members of the National Security Council, the NSC Staff will continue to play a dominant role in the formulation of national security policy into the next century.

What follows is an effort to outline the functional requirements of the NSC Staff, identify certain features of NSC Staff decision-making, examine the international and domestic environments in which national security is embedded, and propose a structure by which the NSC Staff could more effectively execute its various functions. Such an examination is important for heuristic as well as pragmatic reasons. From a scholarly perspective, much has been written about decision-making within the immediate circle of the president. Such accounts have ranged from the theoretical to the anecdotal. There is room, however, for a more rigorous look at the role of the NSC Staff—a look that will help modify or amplify some extant wisdom on the subject. From a policy perspective, a more thorough understanding of the functional requirements of the NSC Staff can help a new administration avoid replowing old ground and taking years to discover what its predecessors already learned by trial and error. To the extent that this effort succeeds in these objectives, it will be useful.

1

The Rise of the NSC

An in-depth look at the National Security Council Staff must begin with a review of the concept of national security itself as well as a discussion of the formation and evolution of the NSC as an institution.[1] For in its roots we find both the underlying rationale that commands its existence today and the deeply ingrained issues of departmental responsibilities and jealousies that determine its course. As we trace the history of the NSC and examine the different approaches that eight presidents have adopted toward national security decision-making, two trends will become apparent. First, the role of the NSC itself is highly dependent upon the psychological makeup of the president in office. Second, the NSC Staff has inexorably emerged as a primary actor in national security, largely independent of the president's use of the NSC itself as a decisional body.

In this chapter, I will examine the daunting issue of the nature of national security and explore the development of the National Security Council and its Staff from Truman to Nixon. The Carter and Reagan years will be examined in more detail in Chapter 3.

National Security:
An Operational Definition

As bureaucratic institutions go, the National Security Council is but a governmental adolescent, a scant forty years old. As such, the dramatic changes that have occurred in the structure and functioning of the NSC are hardly surprising. Indeed, the term "national security" is only slightly older than the NSC itself, having come into vogue immediately after the Second

World War. The all-consuming nature of that war demonstrated to policymakers from the president down that there was a pressing need for an institutional body to deal with the overarching elements of national policy that transcended the responsibilities of individual departments.

But, as popular as the term "national security" has become, there is no widely accepted definition as to what it really encompasses. Such a definition is of great importance because it is difficult for people to agree on who should manage national security if they do not agree on what it is.

In the 1940s, national security was seen primarily as protection from external invasion, an attitude driven primarily by the war.[2] As a result, the original concept had a strong military component. The charter of the NSC, promulgated in 1947, created the NSC to "enable the military services and other departments and agencies of the government to cooperate more effectively in matters involving the national security."[3] Clearly, in 1947, the military dimension of national security was the primary concern.

This narrow definition facilitated the management of national security, and the process was dominated by the military establishment. The early discussions on the composition of the NSC reflected this orientation; in 1946, the Senate proposed that the secretary of defense chair the NSC. This is a far cry from the implicit definition of national security that led Secretary of State Alexander Haig to propose, in 1980, that he become the "vicar for the community of departments having an interest in the several dimensions of foreign policy."[4] Clearly, in Haig's mind, national security was dominated by its foreign policy component.

The definition a president assigns to national security helps to determine the roles each agency plays in the national security system. If, for example, the president adopted the Haig view, the secretary of state would be expected to dominate the national security machinery. If, on the other hand, the more traditional view is adopted, the secretary of defense will have a stronger voice. The third alternative is to view national security as a decisional discipline that is neither primarily foreign nor defense policy. Rather, national security is seen as an overarching, interdisciplinary, dynamic paradigm embracing the elements and responsibilities of a number of departments. Under this for-

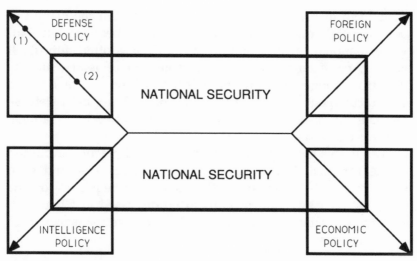

FIGURE 1.1   National security

mulation, the White House emerges as the focus for the national security system.

It is this last approach that led to the formation of the National Security Council in the first place and is implicitly recognized today. But to say simply that national security transcends the responsibilities of any single department provides no real guidance on the supporting structure or functions of national security. It is important to provide a definition of national security that takes such concerns into account.

To that end, I would define national security as the protection of the United States from major threats to our territorial, political, or economic well-being. The national security system and process are primarily concerned with the integration and coordination of defense policy, foreign policy, international economic policy, and intelligence policy and the procedures associated with each of these arenas. This structural approach is illustrated in Figure 1.1.

As is evident in the Figure 1.1 schematic, national security is a series of continual embracing the overlapping areas of separate departmental responsibilities. This is not surprising, considering the widespread acceptance of the overarching paradigm. But national security also entails certain areas normally thought to involve only a single department. On the margin of departmental responsibilities, discriminating between what involves national security and what does not is often difficult. It is clear, for example, that the management of issues such as doctrinal changes in army training (point 1 on Figure 1.1) and the procurement of a new army tank (point 2) are both Defense Department responsibilities, yet only the latter is a national security concern.

Seen in this light, the growth, changes, and practical evolution of the National Security Council make more sense and even seem predictable. Moreover, the functional requisites of the National Security Council Staff, to be discussed in Chapter 2, emerge as essential ingredients in the effective management of national security.

National Security: Institutional Management

Using the definition presented above, we now turn to a discussion of how the United States has developed and refined its national security system. The history of the NSC breaks down into four segments: the conceptual period (1920–1945), the birth (1945–1949), the growth period (1949–1968), and institutional maturity (1969–present). Each of these stages will be discussed briefly below.

The Conceptual Period

Although the Second World War gave irreversible momentum to the establishment of the NSC, the need for such an organization had been identified much earlier. As early as 1919, Franklin Delano Roosevelt proposed the establishment of a "Joint Plan-Making Body" to deal with issues that overlapped between the departments of State, War, and Navy.[5] The failure of that initiative was manifest in the Washington Naval Limitations Conference, during which the State Department negotiated arbitrary limitations on capital vessels with virtually no coordination with the Navy.[6]

Partially because of this debacle and partially because of the rising threat emerging from Germany and Japan, Secretary of State Cordell Hull proposed that the president establish the Standing Liaison Committee, an interagency group to coordinate defense and foreign policy. This organization, constituted in 1935 and composed of the under secretary of state, the chief of staff of the army, and the chief of naval operations, became the first institutionalized group to deal with what would later be called national security.[7] But, as with any bureaucratic prototype, the Standing Liaison Committee did not live up to the expectations of its designer; its members were simply unschooled in the requirements of interagency coordination and jealously guarded their own interests.[8] Moreover, the committee had no independent staff to provide support, continuity, and a national-level perspective.

The war, quite naturally, engendered a proliferation of interagency coordinating bodies of all types to deal with a variety of issues. FDR, recognizing the gathering war clouds, established the War Council, which consisted of the secretaries of state, war, and navy as well as the chiefs of the respective services. Despite the superficial similarities between the War Council and the NSC, the former did not provide for the genuine integration of diplomacy and defense; it was used primarily as a mechanism to formulate wartime strategy. The State Department assumed a decidedly secondary role, and after the war broke out, Hull was no longer even invited to attend War Council meetings.[9]

The first real effort to establish a meaningful interagency body on a permanent basis came in 1945 with the creation of the State-War-Navy Coordinating Committee. This group, consisting of the assistant secretaries of the respective departments, actually dealt with some cross-cutting issues from a national security perspective, rather than using the traditional stovepipe approaches of the departments. But the lack of real clout in the government and the committee's inability to generate issues internally doomed this early effort to irrelevance. However, like the Standing Liaison Committee before it, the Coordinating Committee took an important bureaucratic step in preparing the way for the establishment of an effective interagency body to manage national security affairs.

The Birth of the NSC

In the aftermath of the Second World War, it became apparent to President Truman that the United States needed an organization to coordinate the range of issues that were now being grouped under the rubric of national security. Between the recognition of this requirement and the establishment of the NSC, however, lay significant obstacles, many of which reflected functional issues that continue to plague the national security establishment today.

The primary reason for the difficulty in developing and establishing the National Security Council was that the NSC itself represented a major change in the structure of government and at the same time was inextricably intertwined with one of the most sweeping reforms in the history of the U.S. government. A brief overview of the impact of the National Security Act of 1947 and its amendment in 1949 demonstrates this point. Among other things, the act accomplished the following:

1. It established the National Security Council.
2. It established the secretary of defense and an integrated DoD.
3. It established the Department of the Air Force.
4. It effectively demoted the service secretaries to sub-cabinet rank.
5. It established the Central Intelligence Agency and the director of central intelligence.

Needless to say, issues of this magnitude elicited both strong support and resistance throughout the government. The bureaucratic turmoil was further complicated by the ambiguity with which Truman himself approached the creation of the NSC. Although he understood the need for such an organization, he was concerned with the establishment of a body that would usurp his decision-making authority. Truman emphasized that "the council is purely an advisory body and has no policy-making or supervisory functions," underscoring his intention that the president not be bound by votes taken in the council or by decisions made by its members.[10]

The actual formulation of the NSC grew out of yet another bureaucratic maneuver, the so-called "Forrestal revenge." As the postwar national security structure began to take shape, there was strong support for the complete unification of the army and navy, a proposal that Navy Secretary James Forrestal felt would doom the navy to second-class status. In order to forestall such a development, Forrestal commissioned Ferdinand Eberstadt, a kindred soul, to develop a plan for a national security organization. Not surprisingly, the Eberstadt Report recommended strongly against service unification but also stated that: "to afford a permanent vehicle for maintaining active, close and continuous contact between the departments and agencies of our Government responsible, respectively, for our foreign and military policies and their implementation, we recommend the establishment of a National Security Council."[11]

Because of the far-reaching implications of Truman's proposal, it took two full years for the National Security Act to come to fruition and another two years for the National Security Council, in its present form, to take shape. When finally passed, the language of the act itself reflected the underlying rationale of the Eberstadt Report. It established the National Security Council with the following charter:

> The function of the Council shall be to advise the President with respect to the integration of domestic, foreign, and military policies relating to the national security so as to enable the military services and the other departments and agencies of the Government to cooperate more effectively in matters involving national security.[12]

At the same time, the act established that "the Council shall have a staff headed by a civilian executive secretary who shall be appointed by the President."[13] As envisioned by the Eberstadt Report, the NSC Staff was to be a "Secretariat . . . charged with preparing its agenda, providing data essential to its deliberations, and distributing its conclusions to the departments and agencies concerned for information and appropriate action."[14]

From these humble beginnings emerged the Staff that was responsible for some of the highest and lowest moments in the conduct of the national security affairs of the United States.

The Growth Years

One of the most widely held views among students of national security is that the NSC is first and foremost a product of the president it serves.[15] Truman clearly demonstrated the validity of this perspective; the first created the NSC with far-reaching potential and then insured that this potential was never realized.

From the beginning, Truman had no intention of allowing the NSC to evolve into anything more than an advisory body. Indeed, from the first meeting of the NSC in September 1947 until the outbreak of the Korean War in June 1950, the president attended only 12 of the 57 NSC sessions held.[16] Truman wanted to avoid the precedent of making decisions at NSC meetings, a practice that could imply that votes would be taken and that the NSC would become a decisional body binding on the president. Truman also made it clear that he considered the secretary of state to be first among equals in the NSC and appointed him president pro tempore of the council. Secretary of State Dean Acheson used that leverage to assume control over the machinery of national security decision-making. Acheson first bullied his ineffectual competitor, Secretary of Defense Louis Johnson, and then coopted Johnson's successor, George Marshall.[17] Truman, as a proponent of what Zbigniew Brzezinski has described as a "secretarial system" of national security decision-making, felt comfortable with Acheson's preeminent role on the NSC.[18]

True to the spirit and letter of the act, the initial NSC Staff was humble indeed, consisting of an executive secretary (Sidney W. Souers) and an NSC Staff of three professionals. Within two years, the Staff had grown to fifteen and was grouped into three loose organizations: Staff members, consultants, and the secretariat. Even with this growth, however, the functions of the Staff had not changed significantly; it still acted principally as an administrative arm of the NSC. The NSC Staff was charged with the development of long-range studies, but the primary strategic direction of the nation came from other groups. In fact, the most famous of the Truman statements on national security, NSC-68, was developed by a joint working group from the Department of State and the Department of Defense and did not involve the NSC Staff.[19]

Individual Staff members, particularly the consultants, were creatures of the departments and owed primary loyalty to the secretaries they represented. By 1950, the Staff had been organized into a Senior Staff, consisting of assistant secretaries of the constituent departments, and Staff assistants who were appointed by the Senior Staff. With this background, the NSC Staff developed no cohesion or bureaucratic orientation beyond the horizons of each department. Paradoxically, the Staff members themselves were not trusted by the departments they represented, so they experienced the worst of both worlds.

Moreover, Souers himself was in no way a philosophical competitor for the department secretaries; he described himself as "an anonymous servant of the Council."[20] Indeed, there was not even a formal position for a national security adviser in the Truman administration. In Souers's words, "no new agent without accountability has been established with the power to influence policy."[21]

The failure of the NSC to effect meaningful national security policy was perhaps best reflected in the vacillation and uncertainty that surrounded the Korean War. White House policy drifted along in response to battlefield developments, with articulated war aims changing every few months. In the absence of a powerful NSC, and with strong antagonists such as Acheson and MacArthur, the integration of the various elements of national power and the development of a long-term strategy proved impossible.

By the beginning of the Eisenhower administration, the NSC had taken firm institutional root but had yet to contribute substance. Because of the distrust with which Truman had approached the NSC and the very newness of the organization itself, Eisenhower offered the justifiable criticism that "the National Security Council as presently constituted is more a shadow agency than a really effective policy maker."[22] Eisenhower moved quickly to elevate the NSC to the "apex of national security

TABLE 1.1   Special Assistants to the President for National Security Affairs

President	Special Assistant
Eisenhower	Robert Cutler
	Dillon Anderson
	William Jackson
	Gordon Gray
Kennedy	McGeorge Bundy
Johnson	Walt Rostow
Nixon	Henry Kissinger
Ford	Brent Scowcroft
Carter	Zbigniew Brzezinski
Reagan	Richard Allen
	William Clark
	Robert McFarlane
	John Poindexter
	Frank Carlucci
	Colin Powell
Bush	Brent Scowcroft

policy making" and, in 1953, appointed Robert Cutler to the newly created post of special assistant to the president for national security affairs[23] (see Table 1.1). Cutler did not replace the executive secretary of the NSC, a position that was, after all, mandated by law. The special assistant was an altogether new position; it was designed to institutionalize what had been a de facto national security post in previous administrations, which had been filled by such men as Colonel House and Harry Hopkins. Although the special assistant initially had no formal supervisory responsibility over the NSC Staff, a marriage of convenience quickly occurred; the special assistant needed staff support to function in an increasingly complex government, and the NSC Staff needed a champion of substance to lead it into bureaucratic relevance. Yet, Cutler did not move to assert himself or the NSC Staff in the national security system. He appeared content to remain subordinate to Secretary of State John Foster Dulles and to allow the departments to dominate the process.[24]

Eisenhower took two additional steps to elevate the functioning of the NSC. First, he appointed the vice president to chair the NSC in his absence instead of the secretary of state. This helped insure more equal treatment of the other members of the NSC and, therefore, more vigorous cooperation. Second, and more important, the president himself chaired more than 90 percent of the NSC meetings and made decisions at these meetings. This guaranteed regular attendance by the other NSC principals and infused a new sense of purpose and importance into the NSC process.

The Staff evolved slowly. While it grew in size and contained what Cutler called "some think people," it nonetheless remained primarily an administrative staff providing support without real substance and focusing on coordination and supervision of policy. Although the Hoover Commission suggested that the NSC Staff should "evolve policy ideas," Cutler opposed such a role because it would "intervene between the President and his cabinet members."[25]

In addition to its support of the NSC itself, the Staff also provided most of the support to the two subcommittees of the NSC—the Planning Board and the Operations Coordination Board, which supervised policy planning and execution respectively. This highly structured system lent a much-needed measure of order and integration to the NSC but proved too rigid to deal with issues requiring imagination and daring. Moreover, because of Eisenhower's desire for consensus among Staff members before decisions reached him, the NSC system often provided what Dean Acheson called "agreement by exhaustion," giving only colorless compromise solutions to complex problems.[26] This problem was due, in no small measure, to the lack of an independent, forward-looking NSC Staff that could see beyond the simple integration of departmental positions. The Staff remained fundamentally a collection of agency representatives rather than a fully cohesive organization with strong leadership and a life of its own. By the end of his administration, Eisenhower recognized the inflexibility of the system and saw great value in "a highly competent individual and a small staff" that could orchestrate the national security system more effectively.[27]

Because of its spotty record of performance, the NSC came under congressional scrutiny in 1960. After extensive hearings, the NSC was criticized by Senator Henry Jackson's Subcommittee on National Policy Machinery. The subcommittee's report said: "The Council . . . appears only marginally involved in helping resolve many of the most important problems which affect the future course of national security policy."[28] In a speech at the National War College, Senator Jackson further charged that the "NSC is a dangerously misleading facade," a criticism that sounds remarkably like the one Eisenhower leveled at the Truman NSC.[29]

All of this resonated strongly with John F. Kennedy, who, unlike his predecessor, was a believer in a centralized, informal style of decision-making. One of the first tasks his special assistant, McGeorge Bundy, undertook was the dismantling of the Planning Board, the Operations Coordination Board, and the rigid NSC structure they supported. Kennedy opted for an informal structure that bordered on no structure at all, and the NSC fell into disuse. Indeed, the most daunting national security challenge faced by the 1,000-day administration was the Cuban Missile Crisis, and that was not even handled by the NSC. The resolution of that crisis fell to the Executive Committee, an ad hoc group composed of trusted advisers, some of whom had no experience whatever in national security.

Despite, or perhaps because of, the decreasing use of the formal NSC, the Kennedy administration wrought two basic changes in the NSC Staff. First, under McGeorge Bundy, the assistant for national security affairs "came in out of the cold," assuming a position of influence equal to that of the cabinet secretaries.[30] Second, Bundy's NSC Staff "came to serve the President, rather than the NSC."[31] Staff members were no longer appointed by the departments; they became independent advisers to the president, providing policy options, plumbing the bureaucracy for information and positions, and overseeing policy implementation. Bundy's charge to the Staff was to "extend the range and enlarge the direct effectiveness of the man they serve."[32] For the first time, the NSC Staff assumed an identity of its own and was capable of independent judgments and actions. As Robert Komer, a member of the Kennedy NSC Staff at the time, said, "Kennedy made it very clear we were his men, we operated for him, we had direct contact with him. This gave us the power to command the kind of results he wanted—a fascinating exercise in a presidential staff technique, which insofar as I know, has been unique to the history of the presidency."[33]

The Bundy Staff, by executing the critical functions of policy formulation and advocacy, thus set a precedent for the development of subsequent Staffs. At the same time, however, the requirements for policy coordination and administration diminished, primarily because the NSC itself was effectively bypassed.

Things did not change fundamentally with Lyndon Johnson, under whom "the NSC system reached its nadir."[34] Johnson effectively replaced the formal National Security Council with his Tuesday Luncheon Group, another ad hoc committee that, for all practical purposes, ran Johnson's most challenging national security issue, the Vietnam War. In a bow toward some measure of formalism, however, the Senior Interdepartmental Group (SIG) was created with the secretary of state in the chair. The SIG was a committee immediately subordinate to the NSC designed to coordinate the activities of lower-level interagency groups in preparing issues for NSC consideration and to follow up on NSC decisions already made. But, as the NSC rarely met, the SIG was equally inactive.

The creation of the SIG was important for two reasons, neither of which had anything to do with the management of national security during the Johnson administration. First, it established the precedent of a high-level committee to do much of the work of the NSC—a mini-NSC of sorts. This function was to be carried forward into every succeeding administration. Second, it reestablished at least the appearance of dominance by the State Department over the NSC process, something that had grown blurry since the end of the Eisenhower administration. As Kissinger described it, "The State Department considered this structure to be a major bureaucratic triumph. To the State Department, its preeminence (in national security policy), however hollow and formalistic, was a crucial symbol."[35] This

perception was to become a major burden in the Nixon administration.

Although the NSC remained outside the orbit of meaningful
decision-making, Special Assistant Walt Rostow and his NSC
Staff maintained the roles and missions given them by Kennedy.
Rostow continued Bundy's elevation of the position by becoming
something of a public spokesman for the administration; the
NSC Staff remained strong, principally as a source of ideas and
advice for the president. As with its predecessor, the Rostow
Staff had little to do with the administration and coordination
of NSC activities, because the NSC itself was relatively inactive.

During the growth years, then, the NSC Staff saw dramatic
changes in its roles and functions. In the Eisenhower NSC, the
primary emphasis of the Staff was on policy coordination and
the administration of an active NSC. Policy formulation, imagination, and planning suffered as a result. The Kennedy-Johnson
years saw a radical swing in the other direction. Gone were
the coordination and administrative functions; emphasis was
now on ideas and strategies. This ad hoc approach of the 1960s
resulted in uncoordinated, undocumented decisions that, over
the long term, could not stand up to the stress of an increasingly
complex national security environment.

The Maturing Years

For a variety of reasons, the National Security Council and
its supporting staff reached functional maturity during the Nixon
administration. Nixon came into office promising to "restore the
National Security Council to its preeminent role in national
security planning."[36] Nixon, an ardent centralizer and highly
suspicious of the State Department, sought to formalize a system
under which the White House was clearly in charge. He also
sought a system that would combine the functional advantages
of the NSCs of the 1950s and 1960s.

The chief architect of this process was Henry Kissinger, who
agreed with Nelson Rockefeller that:

> There exists no regular staff procedure for arriving at decisions;
> instead, ad hoc groups are formed as the need arises. No staff

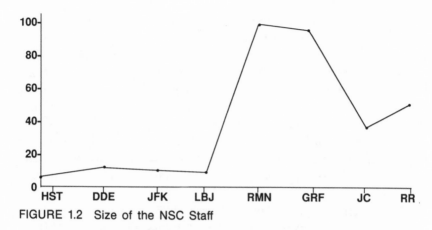

FIGURE 1.2   Size of the NSC Staff

agency to monitor the carrying out of decisions is available. There is no focal point for long-range planning on an interagency basis. Without a centralized focus, foreign policy turns into a series of unrelated decisions.[37]

After the highly idiosyncratic styles of Kennedy and Johnson, Kissinger resolved to restore regularity to the national security process. This he accomplished in two ways. First, he restructured the set of committees subordinate to the NSC, removed the State Department from its "first among equals" status, and centralized NSC and sub-NSC decision-making in the White House. Of the seven committees subordinate to the NSC, six were chaired by Kissinger. Second, he dramatically expanded the size and quality of the NSC Staff itself. Since the late Truman administration, the professional NSC Staff had consisted of only ten to fifteen members. Nixon's NSC Staff expanded ultimately to more than fifty professionals (see Figure 1.2). This growth enabled the NSC Staff to extend its functional responsibilities to such a degree that it assumed the dominant role among the various government agencies concerned with national security. For the first time, the NSC Staff assumed administrative and coordinating functions at the same time it was leading the bureaucracy in the development and articulation of policy. This was quite a dramatic departure from the responsibilities first developed by Sidney Souers a generation earlier.

During the second Nixon administration, Kissinger assumed the role of secretary of state while maintaining his portfolio as assistant to the president for national security affairs. This unprecedented amalgamation of power, although relatively short-lived, gave great continuity and cohesion to U.S. national security policy. It also gave rise to considerable bureaucratic rumblings against the role of the national security adviser, rumblings that were only partially quieted when Gerald Ford appointed Air Force Lieutenant General Brent Scowcroft as national security adviser. As noted by Donald Neuchterlein:

> The dramatic aspect of the elaborate NSC machinery set up in 1969 was the pervasive influence of Henry Kissinger. . . . He wielded enormous power over the foreign policy machinery of the government with the support of President Nixon, who found in Kissinger the person he needed in the White House to retain control of foreign policy.[38]

The Nixon-Ford years demonstrated the maturing of the NSC system and its supporting Staff. Under Kissinger, the NSC became the primary focal point for all national security planning, coordination, decision-making, and supervision. The evolution did not occur, as many analysts would have us believe, simply because Richard Nixon hated the State Department. It happened far more because the U.S. government recognized that the scope of issues impacting on the security of the nation ranged far beyond the purview of a single department and that only the White House could effect the coordination demanded by the mounting complexity of the international system.

Conclusion

Since the end of the Second World War, it has become increasingly apparent that the nineteenth-century model of foreign and military policy formulation is clearly inadequate. Expanding threats to the vital interests of the United States now emanate from a host of sources, including not just foreign armies but also international economic competition, communications and transportation explosions, north-south developmental issues, political pressures from international fora, and a host of other challenges. Under virtually any definition, national security now requires a thorough integration of all the elements of power the United States can bring to bear. Yet, the government has been slow to design a system that responds to these demands—a system that facilitates the execution of critical national security functions.

From this brief examination of the dimensions of national security and the systems that six administrations designed to meet national security needs, it becomes apparent that some further measures are required in order to transcend the idiosyncracies of individual administrations and provide cohesion to national security decision-making. It is to that challenge that we now direct our attention.

2

Functions of the NSC Staff

In order to gain an understanding of the NSC Staff that goes beyond the level of bureaucratic in-fighting and media hyperbole and construct an effective model of the NSC Staff of the future, it is important to begin with an examination of the functions that the NSC Staff must perform within the national security system.

At the outset of any discussion of the NSC Staff, it is essential to first draw an obvious yet important and often overlooked distinction. In many fora, it is popular to refer to the "NSC" when what is meant is the NSC Staff. This is a common but misleading shorthand used by journalists and the like that tends to obscure the difference between the NSC itself and the Staff that provides its support. As was evident in Chapter 1, the difference between the role of the NSC and that of its Staff may be of great significance. The NSC is, of course, a creature of the president; he can use it in any manner he sees fit, as became apparent when we examined the dramatic differences in the role of the NSC under Eisenhower and then under Kennedy. The NSC is, after all, simply a forum in which cabinet-level advisers to the president meet to discuss lofty issues of national security. As such, the NSC has no institutional cohesion, little corporate memory, and no life beyond that which the president gives it.

The NSC Staff, on the other hand, is an institutional body that has assumed mounting importance over the past forty years. Unlike its parent organization, the Staff must perform several critical functions that are driven largely by the diverse nature of the international environment and are generally independent of the psychology of the president himself. The Tower Commission, appointed by Ronald Reagan to investigate the Iran-Contra affair, stated that "there are certain functions which need to be performed in some way for any president."[1] For analytical purposes, these might be called the NSC Staff's "functional requisites." The degree to which any national security structure supports the performance of these functions is directly related to the degree to which the management of national security within an administration will be successful.

The Functional Requisites

There are several vital functions that the NSC Staff has periodically performed. These functions are:

1. Administration.
2. Policy coordination and integration.
3. Policy supervision.
4. Policy adjudication.
5. Crisis management.
6. Policy formulation.
7. Policy advocacy.

The execution of these functions has been the source of NSC Staff effectiveness, or lack thereof, as well as bureaucratic infighting since the maturation of the national security system under Henry Kissinger. Some are widely accepted as the legitimate purview of the Staff while others elicit howls of protest from all sides of the national security spectrum (Figure 2.1).

Regardless of the degree of controversy each function engenders, the execution of all of these functions is critical to the successful management of national security into the twenty-first century. A brief description of each function follows.

Administration

In discussing the functional requisites, it is useful to begin with the least controversial end of the spectrum: administration.

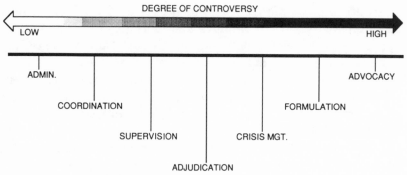

FIGURE 2.1 Functional controversy

Since its inception, the NSC Staff has always acted as the administrative arm of the National Security Council. The execution of this function was clearly the intent of the 1947 National Security Act, which created a "staff headed by a civilian executive secretary" to support the work of the NSC.[2] There seems little dispute surrounding this function; even I. M. Destler, a frequent critic of the NSC and an advocate of abolishing the post of assistant to the president for national security affairs, agrees that the administrative and organizational functions are critical and, indeed, should be the primary focus of the NSC Staff.[3] Philip Odeen, who authored a major study on the NSC, characterized this function as "managing the decision process" and argued that, by proper execution of this function, the Staff "can make the decision process more orderly and increase the flow of useful information, thereby increasing the likelihood of sensible decisions."[4]

Yet, as clear-cut and necessary as this function appears, there are aspects of administration that bear closer scrutiny. In fact, the administration function is best seen as a continuum running from the most mundane of tasks—such as typing and distribution of NSC-related papers—at one end, to potentially influential administrative functions—such as NSC note-taking and preparation of summary documents—at the other. In executing the latter set of administrative functions, the NSC Staff can border on policy formulation, particularly in a highly centralized administration.

To accomplish the clerical dimensions of the administration function, the NSC Staff employs a support group of unparalleled capability. Not only do these individuals have impeccable clerical skills, but they also understand the complex issues with which they are dealing and, even more challenging, the bureaucratic milieu in which the Staff is operating. The obvious capabilities of Fawn Hall, a brief nova during the Iran-Contra hearings, are indicative of the caliber of personnel on the clerical side of the NSC Staff. To oversee the activities of this Staff, as well as the technical details of administration, most administrations have followed the letter of the 1947 act and have appointed an executive or staff secretary. Brzezinski described the incumbent of this position as "the person who really makes the NSC Staff run."[5] The executive secretary also manages the flow of papers within the NSC Staff and throughout the national security community—another responsibility fraught with challenge. It is one of the many ironies surrounding the NSC Staff that, alone among the various staff positions, the executive secretary precisely fulfills the functions outlined in the originating legislation. As challenging as this dimension of administration can be, it is the aspect that receives widest support from the national security system and elicits the least measure of controversy.

At the other end of this functional spectrum, the Staff members have substantial administrative responsibilities that can heavily influence actual policy formulation. Two examples illustrate this point. First, the assistant to the president is generally responsible for preparing the agenda for NSC meetings. Although on the surface this appears to be a straightforward task, in reality, control over the NSC agenda is a potentially powerful tool in managing national security affairs. The assistant to the president, supported by the NSC Staff, determines which issues will actually reach the president and the formal NSC for deliberation and decision. Within limits, it thus becomes possible for the NSC Staff to exercise a bureaucratic pocket veto over an issue simply by insuring that it never reaches the president for consideration. Moreover, agenda items can be scheduled for specific NSC meetings so that certain principals with strongly held views are not present to participate in the discussion. Secretary of State

Cyrus Vance, for example, was traveling when the issue of the Iran rescue attempt was debated in the NSC; he was a strong opponent of the effort and eventually resigned in protest.[6]

Control of the agenda can also extend to the list of invitees. As mentioned earlier, the NSC itself is but a four-person body. But it is usually augmented by persons of cabinet rank who have an interest in a particular issue under consideration. By extending or withholding invitations, the NSC Staff can help shape the discussion and the outcome of the issue itself.

A second administrative task that can influence policy is note-taking. In the post-Watergate era, the White House has been understandably reluctant to tape meetings or even to have verbatim transcripts made. Instead, the NSC tends to rely on NSC Staff members to take notes and then to transcribe them into summaries for the president. The NSC Staff member invited to take the notes is usually the individual who has Staff responsibility for the issue under discussion and has, therefore, more than a passing interest and expertise. This practice, coupled with an understandable lack of shorthand skills, can lead to the practice of "creative note-taking" in which the Staff member, unintentionally or otherwise, highlights certain arguments, downplays others, and in general shades the notes with his particular perspective. In addition, because he is hardly a disinterested observer, the Staff member can get so wrapped up in the dynamics of the meeting itself that he forgets why he is there and misses some key point. He must then try to recreate what was said during his intellectual holiday. This practice reached its zenith during the Carter-Brzezinski years, when such staff-developed summaries were not subject to review by the principals prior to submission to the president. More will be said about creative note-taking in succeeding chapters.

We therefore find that, even in the seemingly innocuous function of administration, the NSC Staff has powerful avenues available to it for influencing the NSC and even presidential decisions themselves. Indeed, as Alexander Haig argued, administration, or "managing the flow of paper," is one of the three levels of real power in the system.[7] Despite these dangers, administration remains a critical function and must be executed.

Policy Coordination and Integration

These two activities are so closely related in execution that they are, for all practical purposes, constituent parts of the same function. There are, however, subtle differences that bear mentioning, and therefore each subfunction warrants separate treatment.

Coordination. This is a relatively passive activity in which concepts, proposals, and policies are vetted with all relevant agencies prior to submission to the NSC or to the president. Concurring and opposing issue papers are collected, redundancies eliminated, and issues requiring resolution identified. Information is shared and a forum is provided for the discussion and resolution of policy disagreements. Along with administration, the function of coordination was clearly intended by the 1947 act. One of the primary reasons for the existence of the NSC was "for the purpose of more effectively *coordinating* the policies and functions of the departments and agencies of the government relating to the national security." (Emphasis added.)[8]

The coordinating function of the NSC Staff is widely accepted across the political spectrum. Even NSC critics such as Destler and Gelb acknowledge that coordination of national security issues is a proper mission of the NSC Staff that is essential to the successful execution of national security.[9] Brent Scowcroft, the national security adviser to presidents Ford and Bush, has said that "the NSC [Staff] has a crucial role to play . . . in coordinating with other staff agencies, the press, the legislative liaison, economists, and [others]."[10]

One of the reasons for this wide acceptance is that, like administration, coordination on the surface requires virtually no substantive policy input from the NSC Staff. In executing this function, more than in any other, the NSC Staff plays the part of the honest broker, one of the essential roles identified by the Tower Commission.[11] In theory, the NSC Staff approaches the coordination function for a specific issue with no vested interests and no position to push. The Staff insures that all departmental players understand the issue, are given the opportunity to comment on a proposed solution, and are encouraged to resolve disagreements. Moreover, the Staff insures that unpopular but valid views are given full airing on an interagency basis.

The NSC Staff has been generally successful in executing the coordination function. In each administration, countless issues have been resolved in interagency meetings in the Old Executive Office Building that proved utterly intractable on the seventh floor of the State Department or on the E Ring of the Pentagon.

Contrary to widely accepted views, however, it is possible to have too much coordination.[12] The Eisenhower NSC is often criticized for being so strongly oriented toward coordination that the issues ultimately reaching the president were so watered down with interagency compromise that they became "only vapid consensus positions."[13] In addition, the coordination process can become burdensome, particularly when the issues being considered do not need full vetting by all agencies concerned with national security. It is probably not necessary, for example, to obtain the views of the Treasury Department (a member of the NSC in most administrations) on a proposed naval exercise in the Gulf of Sidra. Although perhaps an extreme example, it does underscore the importance of judgment and discretion on the part of the NSC Staff in deciding whether a certain issue needs the concurrence of a particular agency involved in national security. Finally, overcoordination raises the risk of unauthorized disclosure of sensitive or classified programs. An elaborate examination of the phenomenon of leaks is beyond the scope of this discussion, but it is safe to say that the wider the coordination of an issue, the greater the chances of leaks. As a result, the fear of leaks is the single greatest impediment to the effective coordination of policy.[14]

With all this in mind, the NSC Staff must decide whether an issue warrants interagency coordination and, if so, which agencies should be asked to provide comments. Contrary to the popular view of the NSC, engendered in no small way by the adventures of Oliver North, the tendency of the NSC Staff is to overcoordinate and to send a document out for comment when it is really unnecessary. The cost of this procedure is excessive delay in presenting an issue for decision as certain departments, with neither expertise nor interest in the issue at hand, flail around to develop a position. The NSC Staff must,

therefore, tread a narrow line between submitting an uncoordinated paper for decision and burdening the bureaucracy with
unnecessary coordination requirements.

The coordination process is facilitated if the assistant to the
president chairs the senior interdepartmental groups subordinate
to the NSC and the NSC Staff chairs the junior groups. This
arrangement allows participants to discuss issues on an equal
footing and consider proposals on their merit. The Tower Commission agreed, saying that "the system generally operates better
when the committees are chaired by the individual with the
greatest stake in making the NSC system work."[15]

Coordination, put simply, is the management of the exchange
of information. The NSC Staff must act as the interagency
conduit for information if this function is to be effectively
executed. The flow of information must be managed throughout
the life cycle of a policy—from its inception as an idea to its
final execution as a presidential directive. But the NSC Staff
must also exercise judgment to insure that the system does not
become swamped with information or that sensitive programs
are not exposed to unnecessary risk of compromise.

Integration. This is the next step beyond coordination. It is
a more active process and may be characterized as the melding
of diverse and possibly divergent views into a single document.
As Brzezinski contended: "Integration is needed, but this cannot
be done from a departmental vantage point. No self-respecting
Secretary of Defense will willingly agree to have his contribution
. . . integrated by another departmental secretary—notably the
Secretary of State. It has to be done by someone close to the
President."[16]

The importance of effective integration stems from the nature
of presidential decision-making. For every issue considered and
discussed by the NSC, there are probably ten other issues that
are decided on the basis of position papers alone. Integration
of these papers is particularly critical in these latter cases.

The mechanics of Staff integration demonstrate the importance
and the potential power of this function. If the national security
system works properly, the issues that reach the president for
decision are those that could not be resolved in interagency fora

at lower levels. They are, by definition, the tough issues.[17] As an issue is raised for NSC or presidential consideration, it is invariably supported by lengthy position papers developed by each department. These are generally uncoordinated papers; the departments correctly consider that it is the NSC Staff's job to effect necessary interagency coordination. The NSC Staff must take these papers and prepare a single summary document for the president. Each president has his own style when it comes to the format and length he prefers, but clearly no president could hope to wade through the flood of papers provided him by the departments. The NSC Staff must shrink these voluminous issue papers down to one or two pages, which will be all the president will probably read and will be the basis for his decision. In preparing these summaries, the NSC Staff must integrate the views of several agencies, identify areas of agreement, and frame the remaining issues requiring presidential resolution.

In this role, the NSC Staff must be rigorously honest in presenting summarized arguments fairly, even though the Staff may have a different opinion as to the preferred option. Time and confidentiality often do not permit the Staff to coordinate these papers with the relevant departments; the NSC Staff may well become the final arbiter of what the president actually sees. A cleverly turned phrase, a dropped adjective here and there, or an omitted but persuasive point can all render inane the most cogent of departmental positions. The integrated summary paper is obviously a potentially powerful tool in the hands of the NSC Staff, particularly if the Staff has an axe to grind on a specific issue.

Thus, as with administration, coordination and integration are essential functions that must be performed. But both have a high potential for being abused by overzealous or unskilled Staff members or by a Staff unschooled in the importance of these functions for the entire national security system.

Policy Supervision

Once a decision has been reached, an effective system of government must have mechanisms for insuring that decisions are carried out and supervising their implementation. Odeen argued that the government is generally weak in execution to begin with, devoting 80 percent of its efforts to policy development and only 20 percent to execution. In successful organizations, those percentages are reversed.[18] Scowcroft asserted that "policy implementation is the poor stepchild of the whole governmental process."[19]

Compounding this problem are incidents of deliberate disobedience of presidential directives by the departments charged with implementation. In an ideal structure, disagreements on particular policy alternatives would disappear once the president reached a decision, and all involved would join hands to insure immediate implementation. Unfortunately, reality shows that the national security system does not work this way. It is a relatively simple matter, in the absence of an oversight mechanism, for a disgruntled department head to simply ignore a decision by the president, or to establish so many obstacles to its implementation that it is rendered meaningless. Richard Nixon reported his "total exasperation" at the unwillingness of the Defense Department to carry out his decision to resupply Israel during the October War, despite his orders to "get the [resupply aircraft] in the air now."[20] After Jimmy Carter's 1977 decision to restrict the sale of military hardware on a worldwide basis, virtually the entire security assistance community within the government set about undermining that policy until it was effectively rescinded three years later. Other examples of this sort of bureaucratic foot-dragging abound.

Beyond these instances of deliberate disregard of the president's decisions, problems of policy execution frequently stem from genuine misunderstanding, overwork, or lack of expertise on the part of well-meaning professionals. But whether the root cause is hostile or benign, policy execution remains the most challenging aspect of the policy process and demands active and involved supervision.

It is difficult to see how the supervision function could be accomplished by any organization besides the NSC Staff. Departments cannot be expected to tell on themselves, and they generally lack the credibility to intevene in each other's internal operations, even to insure that a particular policy decided by the president is carried out. The departments, quite simply, have lives unto themselves and are often only marginally responsive to the president, whom they may consider to be only a policy dilettante temporarily thrust upon them. Dean Rusk said, "After all, the foreign service does not share the view that the world was created at the last presidential election or that a world of of more than 160 nations will somehow be different because we elected one man rather than another as president."[21] It is easy to see how this attitude, reflected and magnified deep within successive layers of the departments, can lead to an almost contemptuous attitude on the part of those charged with implementing presidential policy.[22]

The president must have a trusted national security Staff. The members must owe their primary loyalty to him and have sufficient knowledge and bureaucratic access to supervise the implementation of specific policy decisions. The Tower Commission argued that:

> It is the responsibility of the National Security Adviser [and the NSC Staff] to monitor policy implementation and to ensure that policies are executed in conformity with the intent of the President's decision. Monitoring includes initiating periodic reassessments of a policy or operation, especially when changed circumstances suggest that the policy or operation no longer serves U.S. interests.[23]

This is by no means an easy feat. Even in a bureaucratically benign atmosphere in which the implementing departments approve of the president's decision, the implementation phase is fraught with potential hazards. The press of events, competing concerns, and the work involved often can bog down even the most conscientious departmental staff member to such an extent that implementation of a decision is placed on a back burner. Should the bureaucratic environment not be so benign, and should the implementing department oppose the president's decision, the management of its implementation becomes all the more difficult. Under either condition, knowledge that the president's NSC Staff is overseeing the implementation process provides powerful incentive for the implementing department to adhere to the president's decision.

The policy supervision function is widely accepted as an essential task for the NSC Staff. Both the Odeen Report and the Tower Commission identified supervision as a critical function. Theodore Sorensen, a former Kennedy adviser and a critic of a strong NSC, allowed that "the NSC Staff can monitor and coordinate the implementation of presidential decisions . . . without usurping whatever advisory primacy the president may have bestowed upon the Secretary of State."[24]

The supervision function is of great importance, but it must not be confused with an operational role for the NSC Staff. The Staff has neither the expertise nor the size to execute policy decisions made at the presidential level; nevertheless, sometimes problems with policy implementation within the departments create pressures for the Staff to assume an operational role. In 1981, David Aaron, Brzezinski's deputy in the Carter White House, pointed to the mounting and undesirable tendency for the NSC Staff to become more operational. The Staff "will conduct all kinds of surrogate activities simply because . . . the bureaucracy is unresponsive."[25]

The Iran-Contra affair demonstrated the validity of Aaron's concern and the danger of confusing supervision with implementation. Questions of illegalities aside, the principal failure of the effort was rooted in the amateurism with which Oliver North approached his task. Constantine Menges, a colleague of North's on the NSC Staff, painted a vivid and alarming picture of the whole affair, identifying the utter failure of virtually every aspect of the scheme. He said:

> Like McFarlane and Poindexter, North always seemed impatient with, and insensitive to, the need for a competent, well-thought-out political strategy. North was moving in so many directions on so many details of projects that he often could not focus in a thoughtful way on how to obtain the overall desired results.[26]

Although Menges went on to document North's many personality anomalies, it is safe to say that probably few members of the NSC Staff would have done much better in an operational role such as the one North assumed. The Tower Commission Report extrapolates the North case into a general caveat against a role for the NSC Staff in the actual implementation of policy:

> Implementation is the responsibility and strength of the departments and agencies. The National Security Adviser and the NSC Staff generally do not have the depth of resources for the conduct of operations. In addition, when they take on implementation responsibilities, they risk compromising their objectivity.[27]

The supervision of policy implementation is thus an important and legitimate function of the NSC Staff. It must never be confused, however, with the actual implementation itself.

Policy Adjudication

Closely related to the function of policy supervision, adjudication involves the resolution of issues that arise as a result of confusion about what the president's decision means or how it should be implemented. It is not particularly surprising to note that often the president's decisions are not clearly understood by all, even when articulated in writing. Odeen asserted that the NSC Staff is often weak in "clearly communicating the decisions, and their rationale, to the rest of the government."[28] Moreover, because of the omnipresent fear of leaks, even clearly written presidential documents conveying the president's decisions are not usually made available to the action officers in the implementing departments who are charged with acting upon those decisions. To be sure, these individuals are given oral instructions, but then the "whisper chain" phenomenon sets in, and the final product in the ear of the action officer may bear little resemblance to the president's actual decision. Under these circumstances, it is inevitable that disputes will arise within and among the departments as to the intent of a particular policy decision. This was one of the more obvious failures in the Iran-Contra affair; no one, least of all Oliver North, clearly understood the president's intent, and no one, least of all John Poindexter, adjudicated the implementation process.

In the same vein, disputes may also arise as to the specific implementing strategy to be followed. Unless the presidential decision document gives detailed guidance on how to implement a particular policy—and most do not—considerable debate and discord can develop during the implementation phase.

Under both these sets of circumstances, the NSC Staff must exercise its policy adjudication function. If the Staff has done its job and has established itself as an extension of the president, it can exercise considerable authority in adjudicating disputes within the bureaucracy. It can clarify the president's intent; it can referee between competing departmental views; and it can resolve implementation issues without having to go to the president or the NSC itself. Robert C. McFarlane confirmed this perspective: "The NSA [and, by extension, the NSC Staff] must be a policy arbitrator, drawing heavily upon his personal knowledge of the President's values."[29]

As a practical matter, adjudication can be greatly facilitated if the NSC Staff chairs the implementation monitoring committee. Ideally, such a committee is mandated by the decision document itself; if it is not, then the NSC Staff may have to establish one. This committee or working group provides a useful forum for monitoring implementation and resolving the inevitable implementation issues. In PD/NSC-58 (Continuity of Government), for example, the establishment of an oversight committee was required. This committee, chaired by the NSC Staff, was able to resolve a great number of issues, resulting in an effective implementation of the president's decision.

As with other aspects of NSC Staff effectiveness, the individual Staff member must clarify his role in the adjudication process in his own mind. He must separate his personal views on the matter and act both as an honest broker and a reflection of the president. This can at times become exceedingly difficult, for the Staff member may not agree with the president's decision. Under those circumstances, it is tempting for the Staff member to shade or alter the president's intent and refashion the policy, however subtly, into something more palatable to his own tastes. The temptation may be great, but such bureaucratic misbehavior is most often the root of his undoing. Over time, it will become apparent within the bureaucracy that this particular Staff member cannot be trusted, and he will quickly find himself exiled to the ash heap of bureaucratic irrelevance. More significantly, such activity can also seriously damage the credibility of the entire NSC Staff and can undermine its ability to accomplish the functions essential to the smooth administration of national security policy.

Crisis Management

Thus far we have focused on what might be called the "process functions"—those functions that support the policy process under noncrisis conditions. The process functions are routinely executed under conditions in which departmental and agency staffs can be fully involved in the decision-making process. This implies a certain luxury of time during which reasoned decisions may be reached that draw upon the full richness of the bureaucratic structure. The management of crises, on the other hand, presents an entirely different realm of decision-making, one that is not amenable to structured deliberation. It is the functional area of crisis management in which the NSC Staff is most needed. To be sure, some crises within the government can be handled wholly within one department. NSC Staff intervention in this type of crisis is both inappropriate and counterproductive. It is the more general crisis that cuts across departmental lines, however, that demands the active leadership of the NSC Staff. There is wide agreement on the locus of decision-making under these conditions. Most analysts agree with Brzezinski that "crisis management must stay in the White House."[30]

The word "crisis" is surely one of the most abused in this generation; it is normally synonymous with any event that makes the evening news. This usage is obviously of no value in the national security business. A far more useful definition is that a crisis is an event that: (1) comes as a surprise to decision-makers; (2) is perceived as requiring a rapid response; and (3) appears to threaten highly valued objectives or assets.[31]

The first characteristic creates a sense of bureaucratic drama, and the third guarantees the involvement of the president. Of these three characteristics, it is the second—the perception of great urgency—that has the most significant impact on the decision-making mechanisms. This perception of pressure is exacerbated by a sense of informational uncertainty. There is no time to go through the normal channels to insure that the information available to the president has been sufficiently reviewed to guarantee its accuracy or relevance. The president thus faces a decisional dilemma: He knows he must decide, but he does not wholly trust the information upon which he must base a decision.

Under such conditions, the president's tendency is to turn to a few trusted advisers to formulate a response. Under the more disciplined, structured administrations, these individuals normally comprise the NSC. Indeed, it was to their respective NSCs that presidents Ford and Carter turned during crises in their administrations. Under other regimes, the president may use informal, "kitchen cabinet" groups, such as Kennedy's ExCom that handled the Cuban Missile Crisis. Regardless of their formal positions within the government, the individuals involved in the president's decisional entourage will rarely themselves have ready-made options and recommendations. They, in turn, must rely upon trusted staff officers within their respective organizations for counsel. Thus, an extensive network of interlocking lines of communication is established in a crisis environment— a network that can only bear decisional fruit if it is integrated in a timely and effective fashion.

It is this function that the NSC Staff is uniquely able to perform. No single department could hope to orchestrate the entire bureaucracy in such a stressful atmosphere. Moreover, the NSC Staff is experienced at managing the bureaucratic short-circuits that come to the fore in crises. The Staff of the NSC is alone able to identify who the primary advisers are at the various departments and agencies and pull them together to hammer out viable, acceptable alternatives to present to the president and his principal advisers. In crisis decision-making, it is essential that as many issue areas as possible are defined and ironed out before options are sent to the president for decision. Time cannot be wasted in endless, pointless discussion in the NSC over issues that should have been resolved at a lower level.

The role of the NSC Staff as an advisory body to the president becomes crucially important in obtaining quick agreement on issues and options for dealing with the crisis. Alone among the departments and agencies, the NSC Staff is in a position to speak with authority on those options that the president should consider and those that should be dismissed out of hand. In addition, the NSC Staff is uniquely positioned to see virtually all the relevant information and intelligence and to task the intelligence agencies for additional information as required.

In a crisis, then, the NSC Staff brings into a coherent whole the separate, usually frenetic efforts under way in the departments and agencies. In addition, once a decision has been reached, the NSC Staff is best positioned to oversee general implementation and to provide feedback to the president in a timely manner. Since crisis decision-making is so often incremental in nature, this feedback mechanism becomes of critical importance in steering future decisions. The president must know, almost immediately, the results of a particular action and their impact upon the crisis itself. Only then can future options be assessed and subsequent decisions made.

There is a more subtle dimension to crises that can affect the fundamental development and execution of national security policy. A crisis can serve as a mechanism for overcoming bureaucratic inertia, particularly when that inertia stems from a systemic flaw that renders the NSC Staff unable to execute its requisite functions. Crises tend to focus decision-making at the White House, and the NSC Staff, regardless of the structural imperatives of the administration, becomes at such times a crucially important forum for policy formulation and execution. And, despite the perception that a crisis must be resolved quickly, crises can actually drag on for a considerable period of time; whatever ad hoc working groups were established to deal with the details of crisis management may take on a life all their own. Taken together, these factors mean that a crisis can serve to shift bureaucratic power away from the departments and agencies and focus power instead within the NSC Staff. More will be said about this point later; it is an important dimension of crisis management that is sometimes overlooked.

The formal mechanisms established by the various administrations to manage crises have differed. Without exception, however, crisis decision-making has gravitated to the White House and control over the management details has become the purview of the NSC Staff. Based on the preceding discussion, we can see that this approach is both efficient and necessary.

In general, the NSC Staff, according to Odeen, has a good record in managing crises.[32] But there is another dimension in which the government in general, and the NSC Staff in particular, do not get passing marks, and that is in crisis planning. Crisis planning in the NSC Staff is essentially contingency planning at the highest level. Ideally, crisis planning should integrate all the diverse elements of national power that could be brought to bear in response to a particular crisis event. In practice, however, "too often, we find that we have planned for the wrong crisis; we have not properly anticipated the kind of problem that will arise."[33] Thus, the NSC Staff is usually not prepared for a rapid response.

Although Odeen's assessment is accurate, there are cases in which the NSC Staff has properly executed the crisis planning requirement. David Aaron cited the negotiations in the late 1970s that resulted in access agreements to bases in the Indian Ocean. These negotiations took place in the context of the Persian Gulf Security Framework, developed by Brzezinski and his military adviser, William E. Odom. Brzezinski, Odom, and Secretary of Defense Harold Brown correctly anticipated that a major challenge requiring a military response would develop in the region and that a readily available basing infrastructure was essential. Aaron said, "in what is probably the most high-priority crisis area in the world, crisis planning not only has taken place but has actually become operational."[34] But, sadly, Aaron also pointed out that "it is like pulling teeth to get people to focus on it seriously."[35]

Yet crisis planning is an integral element of successful crisis management. Although the NSC Staff cannot be expected to anticipate the timing and nature of a specific crisis, it can and should seek out areas in which threats to vital U.S. objectives are likely to develop and begin to evaluate the tools necessary for successful resolution of a crisis.

Policy Formulation

Up until now, our task has been relatively straightforward; with few exceptions, analysts and practitioners of national security tend to agree with the list of functional requisites presented thus far. However, the next two functions to be discussed, policy formulation and policy advocacy, enjoy no such consensus. Those who oppose the execution of these functions by the NSC Staff usually take the zero-sum perspective—that, as John Allen Williams argued, the "increased reliance on the Assistant to the President for National Security Affairs and the NSC Staff, generally [comes] at the expense of the influence of the Secretary of State and the Department of State."[36] Henry Kissinger, the archetype of the powerful APNSA, said that:

I have become convinced that a President should make the Secretary of State his principal adviser and use the national security adviser primarily as a senior administrator and coordinator to make certain that each significant point of view is heard. If the security adviser becomes active in the development and articulation of policy, he must inevitably diminish the Secretary of State and reduce his effectiveness.[37]

Implicit in this perspective is the assumption that policy formulation is the proper purview of the State Department and that any effort to dilute its leadership in this area is inherently wrong. Because competition between the State Department and the NSC Staff is such a ubiquitous feature of the national security system, some discussion of this view is necessary. The issue really turns on two subordinate questions: What is the nature of presidential decision-making, and how capable is the State Department in formulating policy?

Presidential Decision-making. The role of the NSC Staff in policy formulation is, in theory, closely tied to the style of the president in making national security decisions. If the president is inclined to administer national security affairs in what Brzezinski calls a "secretarial system," the preponderance of policy formulation will devolve to the departments, particularly the

Department of State. If, on the other hand, the president adopts the "presidential system" and acts "with intimate involvement" in national security matters, then the focus of national security administration will be in the White House, with the NSC Staff having a major role in policy formulation.[38]

Although this distinction is useful from an analytical or historical perspective, in practice most presidents are driven to the presidential system. Brzezinski argued that this approach will become increasingly prevalent in the future because presidents want to be seen as being in control of national security affairs, because an increasing number of issues cut across departmental lines, and because the nuclear age leaves no margin for error.[39] Kissinger confirmed this perspective by arguing that "for reasons best left to psychologists, presidents tend to increasingly centralize decision-making in the White House."[40] To be sure, the curve toward centralization is not smooth, and some presidents are more centralized than others. But it does appear that national security decision-making has been increasingly centered in the White House and all indications are that this trend will continue.

If this is true, then the role of the NSC Staff in formulating policy will become more critical than ever. Nowhere else in the government does the president have a staff upon which he can rely for national security advice that is tailored to suit his philosophy and that responds directly to the electoral mandate all presidents believe they have. Moreover, the large departments of State and Defense cannot provide advice and recommendations that take into consideration all the elements of power available to the president. Except at the very highest levels, the departments are staffed by professionals who generally survive changes in administrations, even those involving dramatic variations in presidential ideologies, such as occurred when Ronald Reagan succeeded Jimmy Carter. This continuity is necessary, and it buffers the country from wild swings in policy, but it also tends to insulate the bureaucracy from the philosophy and desires of the president. Only the NSC Staff can fully meet the demands of a presidential system in the formulation of national security policy. If such a system is the wave of the future, then the NSC Staff will continue to grow in importance.

Capabilities of State. Every president since Kennedy has come into office pledging to restore the primacy of the State Department in foreign and national security policy, and every president has been disappointed in what the State Department provides him.[41] Kennedy adviser Theodore Sorensen said that the State Department was "unwilling or unable to assume its new responsibilities." He characterized the department as plagued by intellectual inertia, a lack of loyalty, and sluggish response to the demands of international pressures.[42] Kennedy had "little use for State and invited Bundy to create a mini-State Department in the White House."[43] Lyndon Johnson handled the State Department with the same disdain; under Johnson, "State had lost ground in the competition for foreign policy leadership, avoided managerial reforms, and continued the lack of planning and direction from the top."[44]

Richard Nixon's contempt for the State Department is widely known. Kissinger reported that Nixon "had very little confidence in the State Department. Its personnel had no loyalty to him; the Foreign Service had disdained him as Vice President and ignored him once he was out of office."[45] While he was vice president, Nixon told Eisenhower that "an astonishing number of [Foreign Service officers] have no obvious dedication to America and to its service—in fact, in some instances, they are far more vocal in their criticism of our country that were many of the foreigners."[46] During Gerald Ford's presidency, Kissinger remained the dominant force in national security even after he became the secretary of state. This did not mean, as it turns out, that the State Department regained all the ground it had lost in the policy wars; Brent Scowcroft, who became Ford's national security adviser after Kissinger, has pointed out that "Kissinger never really moved over to the State Department. He was never in a true sense of the word a Secretary of State."[47]

Jimmy Carter, following the promises of many presidents, came into office resolved to subordinate his national security adviser to the secretary of state, making his NSA act primarily as an administrator rather than a formulator of policy.[48] But, like many of his predecessors, Carter was disappointed. "I rarely received innovative ideas from [the State Department] staff about how to modify existing policy in order to meet changing conditions."[49]

Although apologists for the State Department may argue that the drift of presidential confidence away from the department is due to ignorance, venality, or shortsightedness, the consistency with which presidents of all political stripes have made this move indicates fundamental weaknesses within the department itself. Speaking from practical experience, Leslie Gelb asserted, "Recent Presidents have probably concluded sometime during their first year that they cannot trust anyone in the State Department below the Secretary."[50]

The most important weakness is the State Department's inability to formulate meaningful long-range policy that integrates foreign concerns with domestic political realities. This rather important deficiency stems both from the structural makeup of the department and from historical proclivities of the Foreign Service.

Bureaucratic power within the State Department is normally vested in the regional bureaus, which, despite their staffing by seasoned professionals, are virtually unable to come to grips with the development of long-range policy. Gelb pointed out that Foreign Service officers "neither by training nor by disposition are gifted or even interested in the formulation of policy."[51] This, in turn, is due to the "management by cable" syndrome, a malady caused by the overuse of a telegram network that ties each embassy to its corresponding desk officer in Washington. This allows the desk officer to look over the shoulder of the U.S. ambassador at any post in the world. The tendency then is for the embassy staff to refer every problem, no matter how minor, to the department for resolution. Overworked desk officers and their immediate superiors have to spend so much time dealing with near-term issues that the development of long-range policy is pushed aside.[52] Compounding this problem is the classic tendency to deal only with the immediate issue with little consideration for the long-term implications of a particular solution. Desk officers, urged on by anxious embassy staffers, simply want to get an immediate problem solved without alienating anyone. The result is a series of decisions that add up to policies with little coherence and no comprehensive relationship to any grand scheme. To its credit, the State Department has recognized this problem and has a Policy Planning staff that is supposed to deal with long-range policy issues. However, Policy Planning has rarely demonstrated any real policy finesse or bureaucratic clout within the department.[53] It is not clear that the State Department has changed dramatically from the "antiquated, feeble organization enslaved by precedents and routine inherited from another century," as it was described by John Hay's biographer.[54]

This is not to say that the State Department should have no role in the formulation of policy. But it does argue, from both a historical and an organizational perspective, that sole reliance on the State Department for this vital function will likely result in disappointment in the best case and policy chaos in the worst.

To be sure, the National Security Council Staff also has significant weaknesses in the formulation of policy, primarily owing to its small size and lack of continuity from one administration to the next. By itself, the NSC Staff cannot hope to formulate all national security policy; the task is far too great. But, at the same time, the NSC Staff has a number of important strengths that, if properly employed, can make it an important contributor, along with the departments of State and Defense, the CIA, and others, to the policy formulation process.

The chief advantage the NSC Staff brings to the process is its bureaucratic independence and its presidential perspective. Since Kennedy, the Staff has operated in direct support of the president, bringing an overarching White House view into the policy process. Departmental staffs owe their first loyalty to their departments; the NSC Staff's basic allegiance is to the president. By the same token, if the president is to make sound judgments on national security policy issues, he must have a trusted body of advisers attuned to his specific desires and general philosophy. The departments simply cannot fulfill this role. It is difficult to imagine, for example, how the State Department, with its built-in conservatism, could have formulated the Persian Gulf Security Framework or forged the interagency cooperation necessary for its success. Only the NSC Staff, sensitive to the evolving maturity of Jimmy Carter in national security matters and his mounting frustration with the region, could have pulled all the disparate elements of the government together and made the policy framework functional. As this example demonstrates, the NSC Staff must respond to the president's needs by formulating viable policy options on specific issues and by developing long-range policy recommendations independent of those provided by the agencies and departments.

A final, practical aspect of the policy formulation function of the NSC Staff is the "short circuit" role it can play. Whereas it is true that large bureaucracies are an essential element of modern government, they tend to stifle creativity. Bright new ideas that exist in the lower strata of various departments may not surface for active consideration if they have to float up through the bureaucratic layers. The system is designed for cooperation and consensus, not for great originality. In order to combat this problem, departments often establish "skunk works," groups of bright thinkers with direct access to decision makers. But often these are not enough to foster creativity at the highest levels. The NSC Staff helps bridge the gap by providing direct access to the White House for lower-level staff officers throughout the government. This access is provided through the oldest of all organizational techniques—personal contact. For, although the members of the NSC Staff come from diverse backgrounds, one common feature is that they are all well-connected throughout the government, generally at a variety of levels. This breadth of contacts provides a rapid and ready avenue for ideas that may not otherwise by heard. The system works quite simply: A departmental officer, or even an individual outside the government, with an idea that has not surfaced through normal departmental channels, calls or visits an NSC acquaintance, who may then propose the idea at the policy level. Borrowing from the Jordan-Taylor model of decision-making (Figure 2.2), we may say that the NSC Staff provides the conduit by which ideas from the periphery are able to penetrate the insulating layers of the government.[55]

This is an inelegant and somewhat awkward system that can sometimes cause problems, for the senior leadership of the departments may have ignored the idea for good reason. This

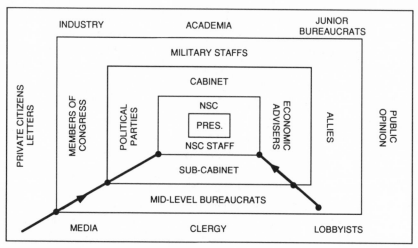

FIGURE 2.2 The short-circuit

short-circuit technique may allow impractical or silly ideas to surface that were properly squelched within departmental channels. Because of this, as well as for less noble reasons such as institutional jealousies, the secretaries of state and defense have sometimes prohibited contact between their subordinates and the NSC Staff. These directives, however, have been almost universally ignored. Despite such problems, it is clear that the NSC Staff provides an otherwise unavailable avenue for original thought.

Policy Advocacy

Once policy positions are developed within the government, the NSC Staff assumes an advocacy role, arguing issues before interagency groups, the NSC, and the president himself, if necessary. It is important that this role be fully understood so that the NSC Staff's advocacy of specific positions is not viewed as somehow infringing upon the prerogatives of the departments or violating a sacrosanct charter. If the president is to be well served, the NSC Staff must execute its advocacy function to the fullest extent possible without subterfuge or apology. In doing so, the Staff must come face to face with its dual nature: As a servant of the NSC, the Staff is bound to present coordinated departmental views accurately and fairly; but, as an advisory body to the president in its own right, the Staff must argue its own views and positions. The trick is to insure that the two responsibilities are kept separate and distinct—a difficult but by no means impossible task.

Not surprisingly, positions taken by the NSC Staff may be in complete concert with those recommended by one or more of the departments. Under these conditions, the NSC Staff becomes a powerful ally, able to argue issues not only on their merit but also based on the Staff's understanding of the president's desires and needs. By using the NSC Staff as a sounding board for positions early in their development, it is often possible for the departments to develop more realistic and acceptable positions, thereby reducing the time spent in presenting politically frivolous recommendations to the NSC and the president. At the same time, this process helps to educate the NSC Staff on the details of an issue, a never-ending challenge, given the necessarily small size of the Staff.

There are three principal ways by which the NSC Staff executes its advocacy function. First, the Staff operates in the committees of the NSC, where most decisions are actually hammered out. By presenting arguments and positions in the committees and working groups subordinate to the NSC, the Staff advocates specific recommendations in a relatively loose and often creative environment. This is the venue in which the NSC Staff can make its greatest contributions to long-range planning. Second, the Staff can present positions in the summary memoranda that cover nearly every paper submitted to the president on national security matters. In this area, however, great care must be taken to segregate and identify the NSC Staff's position from the summary of the department's paper. Third, the Staff makes recommendations through the APSNA in his role as national security adviser. He then presents these positions to the president, either in the forum of the NSC or directly in daily meetings.

Perhaps no other function arouses the anti-Staff faction within the government more quickly than does policy advocacy. Critics of the NSC are often under the illusion that the bright, articulate people that make up the NSC Staff can somehow be muzzled and will not present their views on issues simply because someone told them that that responsibility was reserved for the departments. Scowcroft said that "the President will seek people of substance," and people of that nature will present their views on issues of importance.[56] In order to promote efficiency, the government should try to harness this pool of original thinkers, understand the critical role they play, and exploit the tremendous advantages the Staff can offer to the policy process.

National Strategy

Policy formulation and advocacy have special meaning for the NSC Staff in yet another area of responsibility—the development of a national security strategy. Such a strategy is an all-embracing set of meaningful policy guidelines that steer the development and execution of specific national security decisions in each of the departments. The inability of any of the departments to formulate such a strategy is axiomatic; no single department can be expected to understand and incorporate the concerns of the other national security departments. It is clear that, as NSC veteran Carnes Lord has written, "For the development of the national security strategies and doctrines, the President requires a planning staff that has competence in policy analysis at the strategy level, and at the same time is not constrained by any concern to protect the operational flexibility of the agencies."[57] Only the NSC Staff can execute this function, which is a logical and essential outgrowth of the more general functional requisites of policy formulation and advocacy. Without an active and authoritative leadership role by the NSC, a comprehensive national security strategy simply will not happen.

In the process of developing a national security strategy, the NSC Staff must act in two directions. First, it must help the president frame his vision of the future, articulate the nature of U.S. interests, and orchestrate an assessment of the threat to those interests. This effort should be promulgated in the form of a national security review directive signed by the president and requiring the participation of the entire national security system under the general leadership of the NSC Staff. The separate departments should take the lead in their respective areas, but the entire process should be interagency in nature. Ultimately, the NSC Staff must be the focal point for the integration of various strategic proposals and the development of a national security strategy that incorporates all the elements of national power in the evolving international and domestic environments.

This is obviously a lengthy and demanding process, but it is a critical requirement if the national security of the United States is to be protected well into the future.

Conclusion

In this chapter, we have explored the seven functional requisites of the NSC Staff and identified the unique contributions the Staff can make to the national security process. Even from this brief overview, it becomes evident that most of the objections to Staff functions arise when it is acting in its capacity as an advisory body to the president. For a variety of reasons, many analysts and practitioners of national security are uncomfortable if the responsibility for the development and advocacy of policy does not lie solely with faceless layers of bureaucracy. They find comfort in the myth that great masses of well-meaning government officials, embedded in the intellectual gridlock of the departments, can produce direction and planning for national security in the future. In fact, it has not happened that way in the past, and there is no reason to expect it to be different in the future.

Instead, the national security structure should be designed to exploit the unique capabilities of the NSC Staff and facilitate the execution of its requisite functions. The structure that supports these functions will be best able to produce meaningful policy and manage the complex affairs of national security in the future.

3

The NSC Structure

Having discussed the requisite functions of the NSC Staff, we now turn to the most important of the variables affecting the execution of these functions—the formal NSC system itself. This system, more than any other single feature, dictates the ease or difficulty the NSC Staff experiences in executing its requisite functions. More important, the compatibility or incompatibility of the structure with staff functions will determine the success or failure of the entire national security system. However, it is fair to say that no administration has ever established an NSC system based on an acknowledgment of the functional requisites of the NSC Staff; rather, all systems thus far have been established in response to competing personality demands and perceived systemic inadequacies of the previous administration. This approach has created significant discontinuities between the NSC Staff's functions and its supporting structure—a phenomenon we might call the "structural-functional mismatch."

The impact of structural weaknesses and the evolution of NSC systems to overcome these deficiencies and respond to functional demands can be seen particularly well in two back-to-back administrations—those of Jimmy Carter and Ronald Reagan. In this chapter, we will examine the formal structures of both administrations and then measure them against their ability to execute the requisite functions.

PD-2 and the Carter NSC

The formal structure of the National Security Council system under the Carter administration was laid out in Presidential

Directive/NSC-2, dated January 20, 1977. PD-2, of course, was not produced in isolation; it was the product of the incoming administration's perception of the weaknesses of the Nixon-Ford NSC. During his successful campaign for the presidency, Jimmy Carter blasted the Kissinger model of national security decision-making and called the secretary of state himself a "Lone Ranger."[1] The Republican national security strategy, Carter said, was "almost all style and spectacular, and not substance."[2] He vowed that he would operate a "spokes of the wheel" system under which many voices would be heard in the national security decisional process. In addition, he was committed to decentralized, cabinet government in which his secretary of state would be the leading player.[3]

But, as Brzezinski acknowledged, Carter and his system would ultimately gravitate toward centralized control, with Brzezinski playing an even more visible and prominent role than his predecessor. Indeed, during the last eighteen months of the Carter administration, the Brzezinski NSC was almost identical in style and substance to the Kissinger model.[4]

Unlike Kissinger, however, Brzezinski faced a secretary of state unwilling to assume a second-class status. Buttressed by a State Department suspicious of White House decision-making, Cyrus Vance continuously warred with Brzezinski virtually from the outset, with the advantage going to Vance early in the administration. It was not until the fall of the Shah in 1978, the Soviet invasion of Afghanistan, and the Iranian seizure of the American hostages in 1979 that Brzezinski was able to assume the dominant position in the national security structure, a position he did not surrender until the administration ended.

With Brzezinski's ascension, the NSC Staff grew in importance as well. Although, with an average of thirty professionals, it was considerably slimmer than the Kissinger Staff, Brzezinski's Staff became the focal point for the entire NSC structure. By the end of the Carter administration, the NSC Staff had resolved much of the structural-functional mismatch imbedded in PD-2, largely because the document itself provided the basic structure and allowed enough flexibility for the necessary growth.

PD-2 begins by saying that "the reorganization is intended to place more responsibility in the departments and agencies, while insuring that the NSC . . . continues to integrate and facilitate foreign and defense policy decisions."[5] This objective contrasts sharply with the expressed basis for the Nixon-Kissinger system, which pledged to "restore the National Security Council to its preeminent role in national security planning."[6] It was thus clear that the NSC, the source of bureaucratic strength for the "Lone Ranger," was intended to have a much different role under the Carter administration than it had under Nixon. Moreover, President Carter sought structural simplicity to replace what he saw as a labyrinth of committees within the national security system under the previous administration. "I want a simple, neater structure," he told Brzezinski.[7]

As a result of these perceptions, two organizations subordinate to the NSC were created to handle the full range of national security issues. The first of these was the Policy Review Committee (PRC), which consisted of the secretaries of defense and state, the director of Central Intelligence, the APNSA, and the chairman of the JCS, as well as other cabinet members as required.[8] The task of the PRC was "To develop national security policy for Presidential decision in those cases where the basic responsibilities fall primarily within a given department but where the subject also has important implications for other departments and agencies."[9]

According to its charter, the PRC was to be chaired by the cabinet official appropriate to the subject to be discussed. In practice, the secretary of state occupied the chair of the PRC in most cases, and the PRC became the State Department's primary mechanism for recommending national security policy to the president.[10]

The second committee was the Special Coordination Committee (SCC), created to "deal with specific cross-cutting issues requiring coordination in the development of options and the implementation of Presidential decisions."[11] The membership of the SCC was the same as that of the PRC, with the vitally important difference that the assistant to the president for national security affairs sat in the SCC chair. This protocol was particularly significant in that it represented the first formal cabinet-level NSC committee to be chaired by the assistant to the president; even Kissinger in his prime did not enjoy such formal clout.[12]

Under PD-2, the PRC and the SCC were chartered to deal with different sorts of issues. The PRC was to look after the range of foreign and defense policy issues, as well as international economic matters and the preparation of the Intelligence Community budget. The SCC, on the other hand, was to focus on a narrower spectrum of issues: arms control, covert actions, and crisis management. The basic discriminator as to which forum was to be used was that of bureaucratic primacy: If responsibility for an issue lay primarily within one department, the PRC was to assume jurisdiction, with the appropriate secretary in the chair; if, on the other hand, departmental responsibility was not clear, the SCC would take the lead. The history of the Carter administration, however, reveals that this division of labor became blurred, particularly as the system matured, and in that blurring process, the national security system actually became far more responsive to the immediate needs and desires of the president.

One important implication of PD-2 was that it formalized the cabinet status of the assistant to the president. The PD makes it clear that, in the area of national security policy, the APNSA was not only on an equal footing with the members of the cabinet but, in the case of the SCC, was indeed first among equals. Moreover, at his first cabinet meeting, President Carter formally accorded Brzezinski cabinet status, a move unprecedented in the history of that position.[13] As will be seen later, this issue was to be of considerable significance in the Reagan administration.

One of the obvious implications of the PD-2 system was that it created competitive committees. The PRC was clearly the forum of the cabinet members, particularly the secretary of state, while the SCC belonged to the APNSA and the NSC Staff he headed. One of the measures of bureaucratic power during the Carter administration became the relative frequency with which the two committees met and the issues with which they dealt. In an environment of departmental dominance of the national security structure, we would expect to see more frequent PRC meetings covering a wide range of agenda items. Because the PRC was the functional mechanism by which the departments gained access to the president, an increase in meetings, coupled with an expanded agenda, would indicate a more aggressive leadership role for the departments with respect to the NSC Staff. If, on the other hand, the NSC Staff were dominant, the SCC would meet more frequently with a concomitant expansion in subject areas. Particularly significant in this regard would be any expansion of SCC authority into areas nominally or by precedent belonging to the PRC.

The latter, of course, is precisely what happened. Destler, Gelb, and Lake reported a significant drop in PRC meetings beginning in 1979.[14] Brzezinski confirmed this assertion:

> During the early phases of the Carter Administration, the PRC met more frequently, usually under Vance's chairmanship. In time, however, the SCC became more active. I used the SCC to try to shape our policy toward the Persian Gulf, on European security issues, on strategic matters, as well as in determining our response to Soviet aggression.[15]

Thus, the SCC not only expanded the frequency of its meetings but began to take on issues that would appear to have been more appropriately handled in the PRC.

In light of this history, it is ironic to note that the PRC had several important advantages in the struggle for bureaucratic dominance. First, it had authority to cover a wide range of issues. Virtually all long-range policy matters in the critical areas of foreign policy, defense, and intelligence fell nominally within the purview of the PRC. Moreover, the language of the PD was sufficiently broad to allow PRC consideration of practically any issue dealing with national security affairs. Perhaps more subtly, all of the principal members of the National Security Council, except the APNSA, had vested interests in supporting the power of the PRC. Since the PRC could be chaired by the secretary of state, the secretary of defense, or the director of Central Intelligence (DCI), all would be apparently inclined to consider the PRC as his formal wedge into the Oval Office. The secretary of defense could hardly afford to support considering an issue in the SCC rather than in the PRC without risking the authority of the PRC itself. The structure thus created a natural bureaucratic alliance among the cabinet secretaries and the DCI against the APNSA and the NSC Staff.

However, the PRC also had two significant drawbacks, which, although not articulated in PD-2, provided important avenues through which the APNSA could expand the role and authority of the SCC. First, the PRC, like the SCC, met in the White House Situation Room and was supported by the NSC Staff. This created the strong impression, even among cabinet members themselves, that the White House was in fact in charge of the PRC, regardless of who sat in the chair. In addition, the PRC was subject to the vagaries of the scheduling of the Situation Room, a factor that could be used to delay PRC consideration of an issue. More important, the formal documentation of the PRC rested with the APNSA and the NSC Staff. This role included preparing the critically important "Summary of Conclusions" of the meetings, the mechanism by which issues were presented to the president for his decision. Brzezinski summarized this point by saying, "The report to the President, including the minutes of the meeting, or the option papers for the full NSC meeting, would be prepared by the NSC staff and submitted by me to the President directly. Though the PRC would be chaired by a Secretary, the report on the meeting would go from me to the President."[16]

This role obviously provided the APNSA with an enormously powerful lever. He virtually managed the PRC system. Regardless of which individual sat in the chair, the APNSA had the last word in reporting on an issue to the individual who would ultimately make the decision—the president himself. This reporting procedure caused much consternation among cabinet secretaries; Secretary of State Cyrus Vance was particularly incensed at the system, pointing out that "this meant that the National Security Adviser had the power to interpret the thrust of the discussion, unchallenged even by the committee chairman."[17] This system, however, remained unchanged throughout the administration.

Subordinate to the PRC and the SCC were the so-called mini-PRC and mini-SCC. As the names imply, these were committees that mirrored their senior counterparts, except that their memberships were at lower levels. The mini-SCC, for example, was chaired by Brzezinski's deputy, David Aaron. These committees were charged with looking after issues of lesser magnitude that could be resolved without surfacing to the full PRC or SCC or to the NSC itself. Two issues considered by the mini-SCC demonstrate the sorts of issues it considered. In 1979, increasing Soviet naval activity in the Indian Ocean, coupled with the collapse of the Shah of Iran and the resulting turmoil in the region, created considerable concern in the Defense Department and the State Department as to the security of the flow of oil to the West through the Strait of Hormuz. The mini-PRC, with Assistant Secretary of Defense David McGiffert in the chair, met to consider the magnitude of the threat and discuss measures that the United States could take to guarantee security of the strait. This issue ultimately received full PRC, SCC, and presidential consideration. The following year, the mini-SCC met to consider whether the United States should challenge the increasingly belligerent Qaddafhi in his claim to the Gulf of Sidra—an issue which would receive attention from a considerably higher level in the Reagan administration.[18] The minicommittees served, in David Aaron's view, as an "extremely useful tool both for preparation and follow up."

The mini-PRC and mini-SCC relieved much of the burden from the full committees and facilitated the decisional process at appropriate levels within the bureaucracy. As with the full committees, the mini committees met in the White House Situation Room, with agenda and minutes controlled by the NSC Staff.

In addition to chartering the PRC and the SCC, PD-2 also rather vaguely called for the continuation of the NSC Interdepartmental Groups (IGs) created by NSDM-2 under the Nixon administration. They were to be subordinate to the PRC and their memberships were to be determined by that committee. In reality, the IGs were not formally constituted or used to any large extent.

The formal PD-2 structure of the national security system, coupled with the informal mechanism developed for managing the system, created powerful tools by which either the cabinet secretaries or the APNSA could gain dominance within the national security decisional apparatus.

In addition to the PRC/SCC system, two other formal national security management tools were established within the Carter administration. These were Presidential Review Memoranda (PRMs) and Presidential Directives (PDs). PRMs, which replaced the National Security Study Memoranda (NSSMs) of the Nixon-Ford years, were the basic documents used to generate formal policy studies. The most famous of these was PRM-10, a "broadly gauged review of the US-Soviet strategic balance."[19] Even before his inauguration, President-elect Carter commissioned some 15 PRMs on a host of important national security issues.[20]

PRMs were designed to lead to Presidential Directives (PDs), which replaced the National Security Decision Memoranda (NSDMs) of the Nixon administration. PDs were the primary mechanism by which the Carter administration promulgated its most basic tenets of national security policy and were considered to be of such significance that only 63 of them were issued during Carter's entire four years. In general, the subject matter covered in the PDs was, in fact, of considerable importance. But the import with which PRMs and PDs were regarded eventually worked to the disadvantage of the Carter administration; the bureaucracy began to regard these documents with such awe that the system was reluctant to undertake PRMs or propose PDs because of the bureaucratic and conceptual struggle that would ensue before either document was completed. PRMs particularly fell victim to their perceived significance. They became cumbersome, unwieldly documents on which consensus was virtually impossible to achieve. Busy policymakers sought alternative means to achieve the same goals, and the preponderance of the last 20 PDs were issued without the benefit of a supporting PRM. The decline in popularity of the PRM was manifest in the decline in the number commissioned; the 15 chartered even before the Carter administration took office constituted fully one-third of the 45 PRMs tasked during the entire administration.[21]

PRMs and PDs were the products of the National Security Council Staff. Although the actual work in drafting the studies to support a PRM might be done on an interagency basis, the Terms of Reference by which the parameters of the study were fixed were drafted by the NSC Staff. More important, the PDs themselves were NSC Staff products and were sometimes presented to the president with only a cursory nod to the interagency process. This practice became even more routine after the demise of the PRM process, which at least required some interagency review and coordination.

The formal NSC structure, as presented in PD-2, was a simply constructed system reflective of the president's personal desires and perspectives. More important, it had sufficient flexibility to grow and evolve as the functional requisites of the NSC Staff became more apparent and as the environmental variables changed.

NSDD-2 and the Reagan NSC

In what has become almost an American political tradition, Ronald Reagan heaped great abuse upon his predecessor's national security structure:

> The present Administration has been unable to speak with one voice in foreign policy. My administration will restore leadership to U.S. foreign policy by organizing it in a more coherent way. An early priority will be to make structural changes in the foreign policy making machinery so that the Secretary of State will be the President's principal spokesman and adviser. The National Security Council will once again be the coordinator of the policy process. Its mission will be to assure that the president receives an orderly, balanced flow of information and analysis. The National Security Adviser will work closely in teamwork with the Secretary of State and the other members of the Council.[22]

Even more than PD-2, NSDD-2 was the product of the incoming administration's perceptions of the weaknesses of its predecessor. Recognizing that President Carter had come into office with pledges not to create any "Lone Rangers," President-elect Reagan's advisers saw Brzezinski as precisely that. Moreover, with the new president's belief in cabinet government, the decentralization of decision-making demanded a less activist role for the APNSA and the NSC Staff he headed. Ronald Reagan had repeatedly criticized the White House–centric NSC system and, true to his word, set about changing the system dramatically during his first year in office. The selection of Alexander Haig as secretary of state reinforced Reagan's desire to move back to cabinet government. Haig, a consummate bureaucrat from the Nixonian school of power brokerage, knew full well the potential for White House management of national security affiars and had no intention of allowing this to happen to his State Department. Moreover, his impressive credentials in the NSC, then as Nixon's chief of staff, and finally as the Supreme Allied Commander, Europe, gave him the perception that he was well qualified to act as the president's vicar for national security policy.

Unlike the Nixon and Carter administrations, the Reagan team did not have an agreed-upon national security structure in hand on Inauguration Day. The new administration knew that it did not want to repeat the perceived follies of NSDM-2 and PD-2, but it did not know what to put in their place. Haig moved quickly into this structural vacuum, presenting the White House with a draft NSDD-2 that essentially vested all authority in the Secretary of State.[23] A hurried review of the draft in the White House, led by Generals William Odom and Robert Schweitzer, alerted Reagan confidant Edwin Meese to the implications of the Haig gambit, and as Haig lamented, it was consigned to the black hole of Ed Meese's briefcase, never to see the light of day again.[24] The subsequent and much-publicized squabble over control of the crisis management structure reinforced the split between Haig and the White House and created an atmosphere in which the only agreement that could be reached was to function in an ad hoc fashion. It is no accident that NSDD-2 was not signed until January 13, 1982, a full year into President Reagan's first term. By that time, nearly 20 NSDDs were in print on a variety of topics but none on the most basic of all subjects—how to conduct the business of national security.

Although the articulation of the national security system took a full year, the structure it codified was practiced from the inception of the administration. And, although the principals could not agree on how to present the structure, they all agreed that they wanted to change the role of the APNSA and greatly reduce the power of the NSC Staff. NSDD-2 did a very thorough job of both, to the detriment of national security decision-making.

NSDD-2 contrasted sharply with PD-2 in both style and substance. PD-2 was a concise, three-page document that outlined the important features of the national security system but allowed, by its general language, considerable flexibility. This flexibility proved invaluable in restructuring the system to respond to changing international realities. NSDD-2, on the other hand, was a seven-page document that was so full of legalisms and structural rigidity that it needed to be either extensively modified or ignored when the realities of the structural-functional mismatch became evident.

Even more significant were the substantive differences between the two documents. The emasculation of the NSC Staff under NSDD-2 began with a reduced role for the APNSA. PD-2 was clear in assigning the APNSA certain roles and missions. It specifically included the APNSA as an ad hoc member of the National Security Council, and it appointed him as chairman of one of the two cabinet-level committees subordinate to the NSC. NSDD-2, by contrast, did neither. Not only was the APNSA not given a committee to chair, he was not directed to sit with the NSC itself. PD-2 outlined the role of the APNSA as an equal member of the national security decisional system; NSDD-2 restricted the role of the APNSA to that of an administrative assistant, insuring, for example, "that the necessary papers are prepared and—except in unusual circumstances—distributed in advance to Council members. He shall staff and administer the National Security Council."

The responsibilities for managing national security affairs devolved almost entirely upon the secretaries of state and defense and the Director of Central Intelligence. These responsibilities were as follows:

> The Secretary of State is my principal foreign policy advisor. As such, he is responsible for the formulation of foreign policy and for the execution of approved policy.
>
> The Secretary of Defense is my principal defense policy advisor. As such, he is responsible for the formulation of general defense

policy, policy related to all matters of direct and primary concern to the Department of Defense, and for the execution of approved policy.

The Director of Central Intelligence is my principal advisor on intelligence matters. As such, he is responsible for the formulation of intelligence activities, policy, and proposals, as set forth in relevant Executive Orders.[25]

This array of specified responsibilities left little substantive room for the APNSA, or for the entire NSC Staff. NSDD-2 succeeded in eliminating any policy role whatsoever for the APNSA and undermined his functional requisites in all areas, save administration of the system, by denying him a leadership role in the subcommittee system. Moreover, within the interagency system, he was accorded only subcabinet rank and was assigned membership in Interagency Groups (IGs) chaired, in some cases, by fourth-echelon members of the departments of State and Defense. Within a bureaucracy highly sensitive to the nuances of rank, this degradation of the role of the APNSA translated into an institutional contempt for the person of Richard V. Allen and for the NSC Staff he headed. Haig, certainly no ally of Allen's, said that "Allen was in an impossible position from the start," and this disadvantage devolved upon the NSC Staff as well.[26]

Like the Carter NSC, the Reagan NSC had a system of interagency policy reviews (called National Security Study Directives, or NSSDs) and decision documents (called National Security Decision Directives, or NSDDs). These documents differed little in form from the Carter PRMs and PDs but were vastly different in their actual use. Recognizing the problems of the Brzezinski system where PDs were issued too infrequently, the Reagan NSC was quite liberal in the use of NSDDs—more than 300 were signed during the Reagan years. But the number of NSSDs was significantly smaller than that, particularly in the early years of the Reagan administration, reflecting a certain inability to generate long-range policy studies.

The structural changes in the two NSCs were not limited to those embodied in NSDD-2. Within the White House hierarchy itself, the APNSA was reduced from having direct access to the president at any time to a second-echelon functionary subordinate to Edwin Meese, a man totally unschooled in national security matters. This lack of direct access to the president was perhaps the biggest factor that ultimately brought Allen down; he was completely unable to execute his role as national security adviser, nor was anyone else able to fill this functional void. Thus, as the result of deliberate actions taken by the new administration, the NSC Staff quickly became irrelevant to the national security process, and the functional requisites, for the most part, were left undone.

When it became clear that, in Brzezinski's words, "Ronald Reagan had pushed the degradation of the NSC too far," several readjustments occurred.[27] First, Richard Allen was dismissed as APNSA, ostensibly for the damage done to his reputation by unfounded allegations of impropriety.[28] Donald Regan, the president's chief of staff, said that "whispering campaigns broke into the press and destroyed [Allen's] dignity and, with it, his effectiveness."[29] In reality, this was only the excuse for Allen's dismissal. He was in fact the victim of the system. Allen played the role of APNSA exactly as it was designed. Haig said that Allen was "enthusiastic about the definition of roles."[30] Unfortunately for Allen, the definition was wholly unsatisfactory. He had no intention of formulating policy, when that was exactly what was needed. Allen's dismissal was far more an indictment of the system than it was a reflection of the individual. He was replaced by William P. Clark, who had been Haig's deputy at the State Department and was a trusted personal friend of the president, but was no expert on national security. Clark insisted, as one of his first acts, that he be accorded direct access to the president, restoring the custom enjoyed by every national security adviser since Bundy, with the sole exception of Richard Allen.

The second change occurred when Ed Meese was removed from the NSC Staff's chain of command and Clark assumed a position equal to that of the other senior White House advisers. It had become apparent that Meese's practice of the briefcase veto and his lack of background in national security issues were creating genuine obstacles in the management of national security.

Although these changes helped to stop the erosion of the NSC Staff's ability to execute its requisite functions, they did nothing to redesign the system or reduce the structural-functional mismatch. Much more needed to be done, and slowly, with almost painful recognition, the system began to adjust itself to the functional needs that NSDD-2 had so effectively undermined. Three years into the Reagan administration, the National Security Planning Group (NSPG) was established in an effort to trim the size of the formal NSC and allow for more creative planning. Then, in 1987, Frank Carlucci created the Senior Review Group (SRG), with the APNSA in the chair and the statutory NSC, minus the president and vice president, as members. Subordinate to the SRG was the Policy Review Group (PRG), chaired by the deputy APNSA. In both membership and function, these committees closely resembled the SCC and the mini-SCC of the Carter administration, and they clearly represented a step toward a more effective national security structure.

Even with these changes, however, the system remained fundamentally flawed in that it lacked a strong national security adviser. Each of Reagan's six APNSAs took his job seriously, but none had the intellectual clout or the institutional position necessary to lead the policy formulation process. This left the NSC Staff, throughout the administration, in a damage limiting role.[31]

As a result, the system was unable to recover. It was intellectually bankrupt in the planning arena. William E. Odom commented that "it is difficult to point to a single example of meaningful long-range planning that emerged from the Reagan national security system."[32] Brzezinski observed that "policy was fragmented to an unprecedented degree."[33] Less charitably, another author wrote that there was "virtual chaos in national security, with no systemic procedure for policy formulation."[34]

It was in the context of this acute structural-functional mismatch that the Iran-Contra affair occurred, characterized as the "lowest point in the history of the NSC Staff."[35] Indeed, Henry Kissinger has argued that the loss of NSC Staff clout within the bureaucracy led directly to the affair because the system's structural weakness "tempted the NSC Staff into conducting special presidential missions no one else was eager to undertake" in an effort to recapture lost ground.[36] Moreover, because the NSC Staff in general, and Oliver North in particular, had been stripped of their ability to orchestrate the bureaucracy through official channels, the tendency was to try to ignore the bureaucracy altogether and undertake missions outside the system.

Although all administrations have had their share of national security problems, none except the Reagan administration has institutionalized a system that seemed to produce such disarray and disaster. The most basic problem with the Reagan system, Brzezinski has argued, was "that [the NSC] has been too weak."[37]

Grading the Structures

Having sketched the structures of the NSC under Carter and Reagan, we can now assess the effectiveness of PD-2 and NSDD-2 in meeting the functional requisites. Not surprisingly, we find major differences that directly bear on the successes and failures of each administration in national security affairs.

Administration

It appears that both structures supported the proper execution of administrative tasks, with the practical advantage belonging to NSDD-2. Partly by accident and partly by design, NSDD-2 in practice reduced possibilities for the informal policy-making process that can sometimes be part of the administration function. Ronald Reagan was an active participant in the NSC, chairing sometimes several meetings each week. Jimmy Carter, for all of his proclivities for being involved in details, chose to rely far more on the PRC and SCC and rarely convened the NSC itself. This, coupled with the fact that summaries of the PRC and SCC meetings were not afforded interagency review, created a climate in which creative note-taking flourished. President Reagan's presence in NSC meetings reduced the possibilities of creative note-taking, as well as the power of the summary memorandum; he was actually in the meetings, remembered what was said, and occasionally caught a creative note-taker in the act.

Moreover, the proliferation of subcommittees that occurred under NSDD-2 helped guard against the manipulation of agendas and NSC meeting dates, both of which can be effective methods of killing an issue before it reaches the president. NSDD-2 also established a separate secretariat for each SIG, thereby breaking the administrative monopoly the NSC Staff had maintained. Although normative judgments are difficult to quantify, the structure of the administrative function under NSDD-2 supported a more thorough and honest execution than that of PD-2.

Policy Coordination

PD-2 was rather light on the function of policy coordination, and the Carter NSC is sometimes accused of weakness in this area.[38] Indeed, the absence of an operational structure below the level of the mini-SCC and PRC did nothing to help regularize the coordination requirement. Coordination of specific issues was left essentially to the discretion of the NSC Staff, with the end result being that coordination was very uneven. Brzezinski, Aaron, and Odom have all argued that PD-59, a basic nuclear targeting doctrine, was thoroughly coordinated with all the necessary players and was an excellent example of proper and effective coordination.[39] The decision by President Carter to suspend production of the Enhanced Radiation Warhead (ERW) was, on the other hand, clearly uncoordinated within the system and had disastrous results.[40] In both cases, coordination was handled in an ad hoc fashion, with little structural regularity.

Moreover, the practice of submitting summaries of SCC and PRC meetings directly to the president and preparing decision documents exclusively in the White House precluded effective coordination, even at the NSC level. To be sure, the weekly luncheon meetings attended by Vance, Secretary of Defense Harold Brown, and Brzezinski (the "VBB lunches") helped in this regard, but few formal notes ever emerged from these meetings and fewer still coordinated positions.

NSDD-2, by contrast, gave coordination a prominent role. It called for the APNSA to "be responsible for developing, coordinating, and implementing national security policy" and gave detailed instructions for the establishment and responsibilities of the low-level coordinating committees—the Interagency Groups (IGs).[41] Furthermore, some IGs were supported themselves by full-time working groups that coordinated interagency efforts on specific issues.

This layering and proliferation of committees helped guarantee that positions presented to the NSC were reasonably well coordinated, as long as issues were worked within the structure. As mentioned earlier, the parade of national security advisers in the Reagan administration saw coordination as their first assignment, and each appears to have executed that function with a measured amount of success. McFarlane, for example, argued that "the NSC system must . . . have the capacity to coordinate effectively the efforts of the many powerful and contentious components of the policy making community."[42] The famous exception to this rule was, of course, the Iran-Contra operation, which took place completely outside of the coordination process. But the failure of this misbegotten initiative was due far more to the ineptitude of Oliver North and John Poindexter than to any structural defect in the system. In fact, the coordinated, interagency view contained in NSDD-5 on Iran was that the United States should "continue the policy of discouraging arms transfers to Iran."[43] The coordinating mechanisms were in place; Poindexter and North simply chose to ignore them.

Policy Supervision

Both PD-2 and NSDD-2 assigned the policy supervision function to the APNSA and, through him, to the NSC Staff. Yet each Staff performed this function in its own way; the differences were due to structural differences embedded in the two documents.

PD-2 specified that the SCC had, as one of its major responsibilities, supervision of "the implementation of Presidential decisions."[44] Since the APNSA chaired the SCC, and his deputy ran the mini-SCC, it fell to the NSC Staff to assume a leading role in the supervision function. PD-2 provided the structural hook upon which the Staff could hang its role in supervision. Using that as a point of departure, the Staff built into many PDs an implementation monitoring committee that met under the aegis of the White House, a practice that greatly facilitated the execution of policy supervision.

NSDD-2 provided no such mechanism. Although the directive assigned the APNSA the responsibility for "developing, coordinating, and implementing national security policy," it gave the APNSA no means by which he could make this happen.[45] The degradation of the APNSA and the concomitant loss of clout by the NSC Staff precluded a structural niche in which the Staff could execute this function. As a result, the Staff had to rely on its membership in various IGs to monitor implementation, but here the Staff was but a single voice in committees chaired by other departments.

The execution of the supervision function was thus made far more difficult, which contributed to frustration within the Staff, which in turn led to the Staff's role in the Iran-Contra affair. North had no confidence that the bureaucracy would carry out what he saw as a clear presidential decision, so he undertook the mission himself. Had there been an effective, NSC Staff–led implementation committee, this sort of rogue elephant operation might never have occurred.

Policy Adjudication

Neither PD-2 nor NSDD-2 specifically addressed the function of policy adjudication, but it is clear from the structures mandated by each document that only PD-2 facilitated the execution of this function by the NSC Staff. PD-2 created a powerful APNSA, and the post was filled by a powerful personality. Throughout his tenure, but particularly in the aftermath of the collapse of Iran, Brzezinski clearly spoke for the president; Carter himself said that "Zbig [spoke] with my approval and in consonance with my established and known policy."[46] Accordingly, Brzezinski was able to resolve issues of presidential intent within the bureaucracy.

Quite naturally, the NSC Staff was also the recipient of this implied presidential imprimatur. This made it a relatively straightforward matter for the NSC Staff to resolve disputes and to interpret presidential directives without having to go back to the president or even to Brzezinski for clarification and guidance.

Admittedly, the personal disputes between Brzezinski and Vance, then later Muskie, created confusion outside of the bureaucracy as to which official was speaking for the president. But inside the bureaucracy, there was little doubt amongst those who mattered.

The adjudication role played by the Staff in the implementation of the Persian Gulf Security Framework (PD-63) is a useful illustration of effective structural support to this functional requisite. The Security Framework was a complex strategy involving a host of initiatives and policies crossing a great many departmental lines; it was described by Brzezinski as "the most important work of its kind in three decades."[47] Needless to say, there were many questions of intent and interpretation that had to be answered before meaningful progress could be made. In the absence of a strong Staff role in adjudication, the entire Security Framework might well have foundered amidst bureaucratic inertia. Because the Staff had structured PD-63 to support the adjudication function, however, most issues were resolved by the Staff itself. The Framework eventually provided "a bold and forward-looking statement . . . on our successors' agenda."[48]

Because of the debilitating weakness imposed on the APNSA and the NSC Staff by NSDD-2, the execution of this function became problematic under Reagan. Basically, no one listened to the NSC Staff, particularly in the beginning, and therefore each department was free to pursue its own interpretation of the president's decisions—or to ignore the president altogether. This, in turn, led to great and public conflict between the secretaries of state and defense, as well as to what Haig called the "babel" of the administration.[49]

Crisis Management

PD-2 assigned the primary responsibility for crisis management to the SCC and, therefore, to the APNSA and the NSC Staff. This structural design was the mechanism by which Brzezinski and the NSC Staff finally wrested control of the national security system during the last two years of the Carter administration. The catalytic crisis that precipitated this shift in power was the collapse of the Shah of Iran and the dramatic transformation of that erstwhile U.S. ally in the wake of the fundamentalist revolution. As PD-2 mandated, the SCC took the lead in managing the disasters that accompanied the Shah's collapse— a crisis of national security under virtually anyone's definition. The SCC met frequently, sometimes daily, during the crisis period to hammer out specific responses to the kaleidoscope of challenges emerging from revolutionary Iran. During this crisis, as well as in a host of others, the SCC provided a highly effective, interagency medium for crisis management.

Over the course of the several months that followed the fall of the Shah, however, Brzezinski and Odom gradually expanded the agenda of the SCC to include decidedly noncrisis issues. It had become apparent to the bureaucratically sensitive Odom that the dearth of long-range planning emerging from the government could only be overcome by assertive White House leadership. Thus, SCC meetings became increasingly regular features of the national security system. The SCC's gathering momentum was strongly reinforced by the hostage crisis and the Soviet invasion of Afghanistan, the two events that dominated the last year of the Carter administration. As a result of the administration's preoccupation with these events, Brzezinski succeeded in converting the SCC from a crisis response team of limited duration into a "broadly gauged body, coordinating all the facets of our response, from the diplomatic, the military, and the financial to the spheres of public relations and domestic politics."[50] Deputy Secretary of State Warren Christopher described the procedures as follows: "The National Security Adviser . . . established the agenda for each day's meeting, assigned special studies, chaired the meetings, and prepared the minutes that went directly to the President."[51]

Although the specifics of the negotiations on the hostage problem were largely handled by an ad hoc group chaired by Christopher, the SCC continued to dominate the national security system. This procedure gave Brzezinski and his supporting NSC Staff tremendous power to execute the functional requisites under the aegis of crisis management. Gelb and Lake, senior State Department officials during this period, asserted that "the post-Afghanistan climate created an exceptionally favorable market for Brzezinski's policy views, his penchant for crisis, and his bureaucratic maneuvering. The deeper the crises, the more they fell into his SCC orbit."[52]

No responsibility for crisis management was assigned in NSDD-2. The sole reference to this function was that the "IGs [will] establish full-time working groups, which will provide support to the crisis management operations of the NSC."[53] The NSDD did not specify which IG would be responsible for crisis management and implied a proliferation of working groups with potential crisis management duties. More important, the NSDD was silent on the question of who was to be in charge of crisis management.[54]

This lack of definition precipitated one of the more serious imbroglios of the first year of the Reagan administration. Haig felt strongly that he should be in charge of crisis management (along with everything else), a view that had been shared by his predecessor, Cyrus Vance.[55] The NSC Staff, on the other hand, wanted to retain that function within the White House, operating under the principle that the president should be the ultimate crisis manager. In the end, Haig lost, and NSDD-3 was issued, establishing the vice president as the overall coordinator of crises within the NSC structure.

The drafters of NSDD-3 were careful to require the NSC Staff to provide support to the vice president, reasoning that only the NSC Staff could effect the interagency coordination necessary to manage crises effectively. There were more subtle reasons for the structure of NSDD-3 as well: To the experienced hands on the NSC Staff, it represented a last-ditch effort to establish a formal, structural base from which it could recoup its functional losses. It was no accident that the drafters of the NSDD were holdovers from the Brzezinski Staff and had participated in the SCC process. They knew that if NSDD-3 assigned crisis management to the NSC Staff, it could be the "camel's nose under the tent" that could be later parlayed into a resurgence of the Staff and a reduction of the structural-functional mismatch. The lessons of the post-Iran SCC loomed large in the minds of the drafters of NSDD-3, and the creation of the standing Special Situation Group (SSG) to manage crises was a direct result.[56] To support the SSG, a Crisis Preplanning Group (CPPG) was established, with the deputy APNSA in the chair. The CPPG was active a number of times, perhaps most notably during the planning for the Grenada operation.[57]

One unfortunate consequence of the NSDD was the evolution of the quasi-autonomous Crisis Management Center within the NSC Staff. According to McFarlane, the Crisis Management Center was designed to "conduct pre-crisis collection and analysis of information about likely crisis areas in an effort to anticipate events and to provide extensive background information to decision makers as a crisis preventive."[58]

In fact, it was the Crisis Management Center that Oliver North used as a private fiefdom to run the Iran-Contra operation. It is not clear that the center, disbanded by Frank Carlucci in 1987, ever really managed a crisis, but it did provide legitimacy to North's independent actions. What is clear is that the deficiencies in NSDD-2 were never fully resolved in NSDD-3 and that crisis management and crisis planning never received adequate structural support.

Policy Formulation

Perhaps the most glaring differences in the two structural directives is in the area of policy formulation. PD-2 clearly established an important, if not key, role for the APNSA and the NSC Staff in the "development of options" for presidential consideration. As we have seen, the SCC ultimately became the most powerful policy formulation body in the Carter national security system. A strong policy formulation role for the NSC Staff is what Carter had in mind from the outset, and his mounting disenchantment with the State Department only served to underscore the utility of the structure PD-2 created. As President Carter described it:

> Zbigniew Brzezinski and his relatively small group of experts were not handicapped by the inertia of a tenured bureaucracy or the responsibility for implementing policies as they were evolved. They were particularly adept at incisive analyses of strategic concepts, and were prolific in the production of new ideas, which they were always eager to present to me.[59]

Perhaps most important, Carter appointed an adviser with a first rate intellect, well regarded in both academic and governmental circles for his ideas. Brzezinski, in turn, surrounded himself with men and women of similar innovative dispositions.

There was no such simplicity in NSDD-2. Although the APNSA was charged, as noted earlier, with "developing, coordinating, and implementing" policy, none of President Reagan's six national security advisers in fact ever evinced any real interest in formulating policy. Moreover, none of them was particularly renowned for his ideas, nor did any of them command instant intellectual respect in academic or governmental circles. In short, they were either not interested in, or incapable of, formulating meaningful policy options.[60] McFarlane, as Reagan's third APNSA, summarized this position in 1984: "The current NSC system is not intended to dominate the policy making process. Instead, it must perform the far more difficult task of policy facilitation and coordination."[61]

Advisers of this persuasion cannot be expected to select or use a Staff of intellectual superstars. Although perhaps unfairly pejorative, the characterization of the early Reagan NSC as ideologues and lightweights did reflect the anti-intellectual bias of the entire Reagan White House. The president did not demand from his national security adviser or his Staff alternative policy options to those presented by the departments, and his national security advisers obliged by not giving him any.

As a result, no one in the administration did any long-range planning, nor was there a staff developing policy options from a presidential perspective. The fact that not a single policy review study (NSSD) was commissioned until March of the second year of the administration is evidence of this lack of planning.[62] This orientation contrasted sharply with the Carter administration, which assigned fifteen such studies the day Carter was inaugurated. The dearth of meaningful long-range policy early in the Reagan administration was the inevitable result.

Policy Advocacy

Neither PD-2 nor NSDD-2 clearly outlined a specific responsibility for the NSC Staff to support and argue policy recommendations. PD-2, however, mandated a structure that, in fact, facilitated the performance of this function. The primacy of the SCC, the vigorous policy formulation role assigned to the NSC Staff, and the Staff's exclusive channel to the president all created a structure that allowed the smooth execution of the advocacy function. Indeed, this dimension of the Brzezinski Staff grew to be so significant that Odeen faulted the Staff for overemphasizing advocacy. He said, "Inadequate process management may be a price President Carter paid for asking the NSC Staff to give priority to policy advocacy."[63]

The emasculation of the NSC Staff in the Reagan administration neutralized the Staff's ability to execute its advocacy function. In his book on the NSC, Constantine Menges related his deep frustration in advocating policy from a position of bureaucratic weakness and watching the series of national security setbacks that were experienced during his tenure. This view is shared by others from the NSC Staff. Richard Pipes, the Staff's Soviet specialist during the first 18 months of the Reagan administration, summarized the general attitudes of the Staff when he said, "This was a most difficult and demanding period for the entire Staff."[64]

Conclusion

We have now examined the basic structures of the Carter and Reagan national security systems and have measured them against the functional requisites of the NSC Staff. Were we to grade these administrations, we would find the report card in Table 3.1.

It is evident that, although different presidents will affix their individual styles to their national security systems, the failure to acknowledge the requisite functions that must be supported by structure will result in national security policy disarray. The Tower Commission acknowledged that "there are certain functions which need to be performed in some way for any President."[65] Having said that, it is evident that much more attention

TABLE 3.1 NSC Report Card

Function	PD-2	NSDD-2
Administration	C+	B
Coordination	B	A−
Supervision	B+	C
Adjudication	B+	C−
Crisis Management	A−	C−
Formulation	A	F
Advocacy	A	F

must be paid to the formal structures that create either avenues or obstacles to the execution of these functions.

Given the above, is there an ideal structure that will serve all presidents equally well? It is to that question that we now direct our attention.

4

The National Security
Environment

Any effective reform of the National Security Council and its Staff must be rooted in the international and domestic environments in which they must function. The NSC was initially developed to respond to the international realities that emerged in the late 1940s and to more thoroughly integrate the military and diplomatic elements of national power. Shaping national security in the increasingly complex international system of the postwar era demanded the synergistic application of the various assets—diplomatic, military, and psychological—available to the United States. By most assessments, this principle will remain valid in the future, but its application will grow dramatically more complex. In this chapter, I will examine several probable features of the environment of the future that would have particular relevance to the effective development and execution of national security policy in the twenty-first century. What follows is not intended to be a comprehensive prediction of what the future will hold; rather, it looks at current trends that will dictate significant changes in the structure of our national security system.

The International Environment

For the first forty years of the NSC's existence, the Department of State and the Department of Defense were the executive agents of the principal elements of national power—military force and diplomacy—in response to the threat from the Soviet

Union. By the 1970s, international economics began to emerge as yet another important dimension of national security, and the secretary of the treasury became a regular participant in the NSC process.[1] During the first term of the Reagan administration, the directors of the U.S. Information Agency (USIA) and the Office of Management and Budget (OMB) were added as ad hoc members of the council.[2]

The trend for additional departments and agencies of the government to become more intimately involved in the development and execution of national security suggests an erosion of the relative efficacy of military power as the primary component of national security. It is a trend that has been brought about by international factors, such as dramatic changes in East-West relations, ongoing shifts in the international economy, the proliferation of advanced weapons, and transnational issues of the environment and information. Such factors dictate substantial revisions in how the United States approaches national security and in the structure of the NSC.

East-West Relations

There is little doubt that the latter half of the 1980s will be remembered as the Gorbachev era. Whether the convulsive changes inside the Soviet Union reflect the death knell of communism or only an ephemeral blip in the historical pattern of Soviet behavior, Gorbachev's initiatives have created new pressures on U.S. national security. These pressures, in turn, make new demands on the national security structure. Dimitri Simes has said, "The Cold War brought clarity in adversity. The disintegration of the comforting international discipline associated with the Cold War leads to a new global environment—one that is less rigid but more uncertain."[3]

The pervasive view is that, indeed, the Cold War is over, and the United States won. Most seem to agree with George Shultz that "we have a winning hand; we just have to play it."[4] By late 1988, polls reflected that the majority of Americans saw the Soviet Union either as a "minor threat or no threat at all."[5]

How we play our hand, however, is the major question facing the national security structure in the 1990s. Most would agree with Andrew Goodpaster that, "If the new Soviet policy set out by General Secretary Gorbachev becomes a reality in fact, the whole security structure the world has known since mid-century becomes open to a series of major transforming changes."[6]

As widespread as the agreement on this point is, however, it has not been translated into agreement on the strategy the United States should follow. The U.S. national security structure understands that major changes are occurring but does not yet know what to do about it. Moreover, it is apparent that the traditional orientation of the national security structure and its focus on the Soviet military threat are inadequate for the future.

The reduction of the Soviet threat has two immediate implications demanding a more comprehensive, integrated approach to national security. The first is the possible erosion of NATO and the concomitant reduction in the ability of the United States to execute its strategy of forward defense on the continent. For all of its political trappings, NATO is fundamentally a military alliance directed against a single threat—the Soviet Army. In an environment in which that threat remains dormant for a period of time, the underlying rationale for NATO will come under mounting fire.. A dominant perception on both sides of the Atlantic that NATO is spending billions of dollars preparing to meet a threat that no longer exists will undermine the foundations of the Alliance and may eventually bring about its demise. This outcome will, in turn, result in the loss of considerable U.S. influence in Europe. Europeans have long chafed under U.S. leadership, tolerating it only as long as the need for the U.S. security umbrella remained strong. Changing views of the Soviet threat, coupled with at least the illusion of pan-Europeanism, will make Europe less willing to support U.S. interests.

At the same time, it is not altogether clear that even a real, long-term decline in the Soviet threat will make Europe a more stable place. Latent irredentist claims, long suppressed by super-power dominance, and the entire issue of German reunification, loom as security challenges of the first order. Ten centuries of almost unbroken warfare on the continent do not engender great confidence that European countries, left to their own devices, will create a stable, pacific security regime.

The loss of U.S. influence and the possibility of renewed nationalist friction, coupled with the rise of the EC, will create major new demands on the national security structure—demands for a thorough integration of all the elements of power in responding to the emerging challenge of Western Europe.

The second implication of reduced East-West tension is the increased likelihood of conflict on the periphery of the superpower heartlands. One of the unintended benefits of the ongoing confrontation between the superpowers, particularly during the 1970s, was that both sides took action to control conflict elsewhere in the world, lest it escalate into a superpower confrontation.[7] The lessons of the 1973 Middle East war amply demonstrated that potential, and neither superpower had any desire to allow the actions of its clients to inadvertently embroil it in the sort of conflict it strove to avoid. In the 1990s, however, with both superpowers becoming increasingly concerned with domestic and economic issues, there will be less energy devoted to competitive issues in the Third World. As a result, neither superpower will be able to control conflict in the Third World as easily as in the past. Moreover, as the Soviet Union trims its security assistance programs in response to budgetary pressures, Moscow's ability to influence radical regimes will also decline. The Soviet withdrawal from Afghanistan, the Cuban disengagement from Angola, and Gorbachev's pledge to halt military aid to Nicaragua all suggest, as Simes argued, that Moscow's "romance with the Third World is over."[8] A substantial decline in superpower influence in the Third World, coupled with the mounting military capabilities of many countries on the periphery, could well result in greater international violence in the twenty-first century than we have seen in the twentieth. The United States could be forced to respond to these challenges.

These emerging realities, whatever their durability, present major challenges to the national security structure and require a new approach to the decisional process. As Brzezinski said, "The systemic crisis of the Soviet world is the new and centrally important reality confronting Western policy in east-west relations. Responding to that crisis will require a comprehensive and long-term Western strategy. Such a strategy currently does not exist."[9]

The ability of the United States to fashion such a strategy will largely be determined by the national security structure emplaced in the future. Bright minds and new ideas are, in themselves, insufficient if they are smothered by an archaic national security system. Structural reform is essential if the United States is to respond to the new international environment.

The Decline of Military Utility

Michael Handel, a scholar at the US Army War College, has argued that "A rational cost-benefit type of analysis leads one to conclude that the days of direct use of power by the super-powers have almost come to an end."[10] Although one might argue with this rather dramatic claim, it appears undeniable that the application of military force has lost its role as the primary instrument of mutual influence between the superpowers and their respective alliance structures. This is not exclusively a function of reduced political tensions; it grows predominantly from the destructive powers of the superpowers' nuclear arsenals. Certainly, the strategic nuclear forces of the Soviet Union and the United States, and the conventional forces to which they are attached, have served as agents of stability for at least three decades. But, at the same time, the ability of either superpower to credibly challenge the other with military force is highly suspect.

Moreover, numerous national security challenges have emerged in which neither superpower has been able to wield its military might with real effectiveness. Vietnam and Afghanistan come to mind as immediate examples, but others abound. Caspar Weinberger, certainly no pacifist, has presented six criteria for the commitment of U.S. forces—criteria which, by their very nature, confirm an extreme reluctance on the part of the United States to use the military instrument of power.[11] Other instruments of power have assumed new importance and, relative to military power, have grown in utility.

Perhaps nowhere is this phenomenon more clearly evident than in the case of the Soviet Union of Mikhail Gorbachev.

Recognition of the waning utility of military power when compared to other instruments was the key to the success Mikhail Gorbachev enjoyed in his diplomatic offensive against the West during his initial five years in power. As Richard Nixon pointed out, "He has substituted the wiles of diplomacy for the threat of force . . . and, as a result, he has made more progress toward the traditional Soviet objective of dividing the NATO alliance than any of his predecessors."[12]

To a world used to ham-handed Soviet diplomacy rooted in its military machine, this new Soviet approach resonated strongly in the West and created significant divisions within the Alliance. Issues such as the modernization of the LANCE missile system were symptomatic of Gorbachev's success in presenting a new and fundamentally benign image of the Soviet Union.

But the success of the public diplomacy offensive was only a fortuitous by-product of a basic realignment of Soviet priorities driven by economic necessity. Most analysts agree with Robert Kaiser that "The rhetoric of Soviet reform emphasizes renewal and progress, but the facts that made reform necessary describe failure—the failure of the Soviet system. . . . The failure is a fact, while the reforms—at least the practical ones affecting the economic life of the country—remain just a hope."[13]

In essence, Gorbachev's Soviet Union faced the necessity of paying the price for Brezhnev's drive for superpower status— a drive that rode the developmental monorail of military power. But, as has become obvious to Gorbachev and, indeed, to the entire world, military power alone is insufficient to guarantee a continued role of prominence in the twenty-first century. Nixon said that "Gorbachev's goal is . . . to make the Soviet Union a superpower not just in military but also in economic and political terms."[14]

Soviet leaders have acknowledged the importance of a redistribution of priorities. Soviet economist Yegor Gaidan said, "There must be a serious reduction in the absolute magnitude of defense 'outlays" in order to resolve the economic morass.[15] And Gorbachev himself pronounced that "Perestroika is our last chance. If we stop, it will be our death."[16] Indeed, the entire system of arms control initiatives and unilateral reductions that emanated from Moscow in 1988 and 1989 appear to be driven at least as much by economic and political necessity as by a desire to live in a peaceful world.

Moreover, the Soviet military bore the brunt of the blame for many of the problems within the Soviet system. Wholesale leadership changes within the Soviet Armed Forces reflected general dissatisfaction with the attitude of the senior commanders, who are blamed for such problems as the adverse fallout from the SS-20 deployment, the Reagan defense buildup, and the embarrassment of the Krasnoyarsk radar.[17]

The extent to which Gorbachev is successful in his reforms—and the challenges are daunting indeed—will shape the way the Soviet Union is perceived in the years to come. Obviously, any country with 15,000 nuclear warheads and 5 million men and women under arms can never be ignored, but Soviet military might must be supplemented by economic and political clout if Moscow's superpower status is to remain firm into the future.

Lest we end up subscribing to Handel's view in its entirety, however, it is important to recognize that the use of military force has not disappeared altogether as an instrument of national policy. Weinberger's conditions are difficult to meet, but not impossible. The invasion of Grenada, the punitive raids on Libya, and the 1989 invasion of Panama demonstrate that the United States has not eschewed the use of force. A direct confrontation with the Soviet Union on the central front or in a strategic nuclear exchange appears remote in the 1990s, but rising violence on the periphery of the superpowers may require the use of armed forces in the future. It is a widely accepted thesis that low-intensity conflict (LIC) will be the primary source of international violence in the next century and must become a central focus of our national security strategy. As outlined in Ronald Reagan's last report to the Congress on national security strategy, "The balanced application of the various elements of national power is necessary to protect US interests in low intensity conflicts."[18]

More challenging than the LIC applications of military force, the United States must still consider the possibility of a military confrontation with the Soviet Union. It is perhaps premature to declare the Cold War ended when the long-term domestic stability of one of the two principal players is very much at issue. Handel said, "The trends I have identified [away from military power] could conceivably be impeded by illogical or fanatical behavior," and this is the very state of affairs in which the Soviet Union could find itself in the 1990s.[19] Acts of aggression against the United States or Western Europe that seemed inconceivable in the 1970s could well be acted out by a Soviet empire in collapse. Kissinger pointed out that "The one thing that cannot occur is a continuation of the status quo. It will either disintegrate under pressure of events or it will be reshaped by a constructive America policy."[20] From this perspective, it may well be that the traditional U.S. strategic principles of containment, deterrence, flexible response, coalition warfare, and forward defense remain necessary into the twenty-first century. The national security structure must be sufficiently resilient to recognize and act upon this scenario.

The Rise of Economics

The requirements of diversified power being learned in the Soviet Union also apply to the United States, although we have long been a multidimensional power and so the problems stand out less starkly. Helmut Schmidt pointed out that, alone among the nations of the world, the United States is an economic as well as a military superpower. He warned against the dangers of allowing the U.S. economic stature to wane.[21]

This is a popular theme today and one that warrants serious attention. But whether one accepts the declinist arguments of Paul Kennedy or subscribes to the rebuttals of Samuel Huntington, Charles A. Kupchan, and others, it is clear that we pay insufficient attention to the economics of national security.[22] That neglect is evident in the structural orientation of the NSC and the relative weakness of the international economics section within the NSC Staff. With several notable exceptions, such as Ambassador Henry Owen, who became a prominent adviser on international economics in the Brzezinski NSC, there have been few examples of consistent quality in any of the staffs concerned with the development and execution of viable international economic policy have been inconsistent. Moreover, there has been virtually no attention paid to the integration of the economic element of national power with other strategies.[23] Fundamental structural deficiencies continue at the same time that dramatic shifts in the global economy are bringing about a new and complicating dimension to national security.

Recognition of this burgeoning economic phenomenon began in the early 1970s when the oil embargo brought the issue sharply into focus. The 1973 Arab-Israeli War demonstrated that a militarily impotent group of countries—OPEC—could threaten the national security of the strongest alliance in the world— NATO. This was a unidimensional and short-lived threat, but it presaged the rise of world powers such as Japan and South Korea that have genuine economic clout but negligible military capabilities. The fact that these countries rest under the military umbrella of the United States only slightly mitigates the significance of their economic power. Japan, in the late 1980s, became the world's largest creditor nation with the potential for commensurate political power. In a world where money talks, the message of the future has great segments written in Japanese. The ability of the United States to manage the emerging economic challenges to its national security will test the national security structure as never before.

Equally daunting and even more complex are the challenges of managing U.S.-European relations in the post-1992 environment. Although the structure and attitude of the EC remain uncertain, the United States must be prepared for a new, multidimensional relationship in which the Europeans are not only our allies in NATO but also our competitors in international markets. Lionel Olmer, vice chairman of the U.S. Chamber of Commerce Committee on European Integration, said that "1992 represents today's single most important challenge to American trading interests. No other issue places a greater demand for cooperation between the US government and the private sector."[24] This issue, like the question of credits to the Soviet Union, crystallizes the divergence of interests between business and the national security structure. Some business leaders have pointed out that "what is good for business broadly may not be good for the country" in the global economic environment of the future.[25]

In addition, there will certainly be political and security implications of an economic union in Europe. As French Defense Minister Jean-Pierre Chevenement said, "It is now clear that 1992 will mark an important step in Europe's construction, and international events are encouraging us to take our own security into our own hands."[26] Indeed, if the Soviet threat continues to abate in the 1990s, latent economic competition, held in check by the need for the West to cooperate on security issues, may be expected to blossom. This effect, in turn, will pose major new national security challenges for the United States. The 1988 furor over U.S. hormone-fed beef and the subsequent tariff skirmishes with Europe may well be precursors of the future challenges the United States faces in its relationships with the other great economic powers. In a similar vein, the heated debate over the joint U.S.-Japanese development of an advanced fighter aircraft (the FSX) demonstrated the burgeoning interrelationship between economic and military considerations in the national security equation and the need for a broader view of the global security environment. Strategist Edward Luttwak argued that "Leaders of the industrialized world must act now to construct a new system of economic cooperation that could stand on its own and not lean on the imperatives of resisting the Soviet threat."[27]

On the opposite side of the ledger, we find the fledgling democracies of Latin America buried under a mountain of unmanageable debt, which amounted to some $420 billion in 1988. Collapse of these economies would almost certainly result in political chaos and a return to anarchy in a region that Ronald Reagan described as "inextricably linked to . . . our own territorial security."[28] Resolution of the debt problem is thus an important ingredient in an effective national security strategy, yet it is far afield from the sorts of issues with which the NSC has traditionally dealt. These developments across the entire spectrum of international economics have important organizational implications for our national security structure.

Proliferation

The factors mentioned above imply that the world is becoming truly multipolar and that national security is becoming truly multifaceted, conditions long posited in the academic community but, until now, having only marginal operational impact. With the proliferation of nuclear and chemical weapons, and the ability to deliver these weapons over great distances, multipolarity has assumed a new and dangerous dimension. In the post-war era, only one adversary has had the ability to inflict significant damage on the United States. But in the 1990s, the prospect of chemical weapons plants in Libya, plutonium production facilities in Iraq, and the acquisition of missile delivery systems by half a dozen countries enormously complicate the U.S. national security calculus. The superpowers and their alliances are in no small measure responsible for much of this proliferation. France built the Iraqi reactor; German firms helped construct the Libyan chemical plant, and the Soviet Union sold long-range bombers to Libya.

The proliferation of sophisticated weapons extends beyond nuclear and chemical systems; the image of LIC in the Third World as conflict limited to black pajama–clad guerrillas armed only with AK-47s is increasingly dangerous and inaccurate. As the Arabs and Israelis have amply demonstrated and the Iraqis and Iranians have underscored, huge tank battles are no longer the exclusive purview of the central front. If we accept that the most likely scenario will call for the United States to apply its military power in the Third World, the proliferation of sophisticated conventional capabilities has serious implications for force structuring; it is no longer sufficient to assume that light forces alone will be capable of securing U.S. objectives in non-Soviet contingencies.

Although international efforts have been made, with varying degrees of success, to control the spread of nuclear and chemical weapons, no real attempts have been made to come to grips with the spread of conventional capabilities. To be sure, the Carter administration made a rather half-hearted effort to negotiate a bilateral agreement with the Soviet Union on conventional arms transfers and imposed some unilateral restraints on the United States, but these efforts soon evaporated.[29] Moreover, it is no longer clear that the superpowers and their allies can control the spread of conventional arms; defense industries in such countries as Brazil, Argentina, China, Israel, South Africa,

India, and many other countries are showing remarkable capabilities to produce high-quality weapons for an eager international market.

It appears, then, that conflict in the Third World will grow in scope and magnitude and could, in the 1990s, come to embrace weapons of mass destruction. This is a very real possibility that the United States must consider in its long-range national security planning.

Drugs

A 1988 poll showed that a majority of Americans considers drugs to be the most significant threat to the national security of the United States.[30] Because the drug problem is only in the wildest of imaginations linked to the Soviet Union, it has become an instructive example of the expanding scope of national security issues. Furthermore, it is a threat for which the military is only marginally effective; the battles of the war on drugs cannot be won with firepower or maneuver. The drug problem is fundamentally rooted in the morals of American society and the economic rewards for drug production. It is an issue that transcends the historical boundary between national security and domestic affairs and can only be addressed by the effective integration and employment of all the elements of national power. Like so many other issues in contemporary national security affairs, the drug problem demonstrates the need for a national security structure that goes far beyond past definitions. The national security system must be as responsive to these sorts of issues as it is to the deployment of the SS-24 by the Soviet Union.

International Terrorism

Increasingly tied to the drug trade, international terrorism has become a major source of global instability. The ability of groups or nations to hold the United States hostage to acts of terrorism is well-documented and has provided considerable incentive to continue these practices. In the 1970s and early 1980s, international terrorism was a national security annoyance, only effective against the United States because of our unique attachment to the lives of our citizens. In the future, the threat will become more substantial, particularly in light of the rising connection between terrorism and the drug trade and the proliferation of chemical weapons. Terrorist elements in South America have forged links to drug producers, creating a dangerous alliance of fanaticism and money. The cornucopia of drug money increasingly available to terrorists will expand their ability to perpetrate acts of international violence even further. This, coupled with an ever-expanding international arms market, has grave potential for creating instability in the future. Of even greater concern, the spread of chemical production capabilities has created the possibility that terrorist groups could gain access to weapons of mass destruction. The specter of terrorist organizations releasing nerve gas in crowded urban areas could well cause major concessions to be made—concessions that have been unthinkable up to now. This is, unfortunately, a very real possibility and one with which the national security system must be prepared to deal.

The Environment

Jessica Tuchman Matthews has argued that "Global developments now suggest the need for (a) broader definition of national security to include resource, environmental, and demographic issues."[31] In this regard, issues such as the greenhouse effect, deforestation, ozone depletion, and population growth, once thought only appropriate for the irresponsible left, now command a more prominent position in the national security equation. The fragility of the planet, coupled with short-term exploitation, particularly in the Third World, have the potential to threaten the national security of the United States in the future. These environmental issues, once disparagingly called "globaloney" on the NSC Staff, must in the future be treated more seriously. This new outlook, in turn, requires a more comprehensive capability for the National Security Council and its supporting staff.

Information

The radical expansion of information networks throughout the world will continue to change the way national security is executed and managed. The governmental monopoly over satellite imagery, for example, no longer exists; the French commercial SPOT satellite now provides coverage of much of the world's surface to the highest bidder. Even the Soviet Union is now in the market; declassified Soviet satellite shots are now available for sale throughout the world.[32] CNN and its clones now reach virtually the entire globe and cover news events as they develop. Technology is making "government in the sunshine" more real every day. As Walt Wriston asserted, "The growing inability of sovereign governments to regulate their affairs in the information age will have profound foreign policy implications."[33]

This development can be both a strength and a vulnerability. Richard Nixon has argued that "Radio Free Europe has been one of the most effective programs in the east-west struggle."[34] At the same time, however, it is clear that the ability of the United States to execute surprise or covert operations has been greatly reduced; during the 1988 secret deployment to Honduras, American paratroopers found themselves greeted at the supposedly secure landing zone by a CNN camera crew. This sort of reality implies that a broader operational application of the concept of national security and a new approach to covert actions are needed.

This brief list of factors in the international environment is by no means all-inclusive, but it does demonstrate the rising complexity of national security. From a structural perspective, it is ironic and probably predictable that our current national security system is best constructed to focus on the military instrument of national power at the very time when the need for other instruments is growing. It is clear, from the international environment alone, that the national security system must change in response to the ebb and flow of the multidimensional threats we are facing.

When we examine the emerging international milieu, we find that the challenges to the national security of the United States may well become far more complex than those we faced in the 1980s and infinitely more so than those that led to the establishment of the NSC in the first place. Only through a thorough and imaginative integration of the elements of national power and a restructuring of the national security system can the

United States cope with the demands it will face in the twenty-first century.

The Domestic Environment

Whether illusory or real, there has been a historical dividing line between national security affairs and domestic issues, and the structure of the bureaucracy has reflected this conceptual separation. In the 1970s and 1980s, however, this situation obviously changed. It is now clear that, as Jessica Tuchman Matthews argued, "the once sharp dividing line between foreign and domestic policy is blurred."[35] It is debatable whether the practical line between the two was ever really that sharp, but it appears indisputable that domestic considerations are playing an increasingly prominent role in national security planning and execution. It is also clear that the NSC Staff has not kept pace with the rise of the domestic component of national security, and as a result, presidents find themselves confronted by unanticipated, domestically based problems in the execution of national security policy. Although the conundrum between national security and domestic policy is complex, three interrelated areas warrant specific mention: the economy, industry, and Congress.

The Economy

National security is expensive. This would seem to be old news, but not since the Eisenhower era has the cost of national security been so hotly debated. Indeed, the budgets of the 1990s may well shape national strategy more than any other single factor. The debate centers on two factors—the almost unimaginable cost of modernizing our armed forces, and a widely held consensus among the American people that the budget deficit is the number one problem within the United States. It has been widely accepted that the defense budget is responsible for the deficit, although, in fact, the defense budget has not grown as a percent of GNP over the past twenty years (see Figure 4.1).

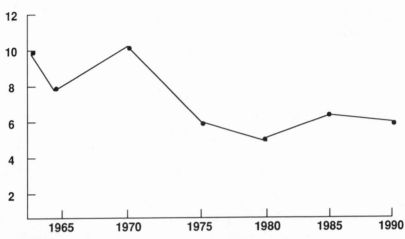

FIGURE 4.1   Defense outlays as a percentage of GNP

National security appears to be more the fall guy than the villain in the deficit drama; the growth of non–defense spending, largely in the form of entitlement programs, coupled with the steadfast refusal of the Reagan and Bush administrations to raise taxes, are the real culprits. Nonetheless, it is defense that has been the primary bill payer for various deficit reduction plans and congressional-executive agreements. Even during the so-called Reagan defense build-up, the defense budget experienced a real decline during four of the eight years.

Absent some major change in the external threat environment, it seems that the military component of our national security strategy will be largely determined in the future by the size of the defense budget, rather than the other way around. As much as strategists in the executive branch may gnash their teeth over this situation, it is a reality that must be accommodated. The effort to rationalize national security strategy with budgetary constraints must be a government-wide task and, as such, should be led by the NSC Staff. As enormous as it is, however, the defense budget is but one aspect of the economics of national security. Almost lost in the debate over the defense budget, for example, is the issue of security assistance. The ability of the United States to assist other governments in their own security is a powerful tool that can be wielded with great effectiveness.

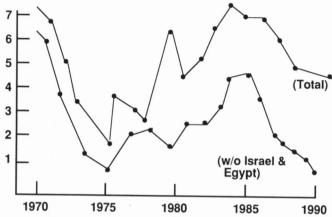

FIGURE 4.2   Security assistance (FMS credits and MAP)

Yet security assistance virtually disappeared in the late 1980s, particularly when aid programs to Egypt and Israel are factored out (see Figure 4.2).

At the same time that security assistance has become a budgetary bête noire, there have been important examples of how security assistance can play a critical, and relatively inexpensive, role in overall national security. In the late 1970s, the NSC Staff led an effort to develop a basing infrastructure in the Indian Ocean to facilitate the projection of U.S. power into the region. At the cost of relatively modest security assistance programs, agreements were reached with Kenya, Somalia, and Oman that allowed the United States access to regional facilities. These proved of great value when regional crises arose requiring the commitment, in one form or another, of U.S. forces.[36]

Part of the reason for the demise of security assistance has been the absence of a powerful advocate for such programs within the government and the inability to integrate security assistance programs with the more general national security budget. Security assistance programs have been developed as ad hoc mechanisms to address specific issues, such as the Israeli-Egyptian peace process and the war in El Salvador, but not as elements of an integrated national security strategy. If the United States is to use its diminishing national security budget to maximum advantage, security assistance must assume a more prominent role. In a far-reaching, if largely ignored, study on U.S. national security, the Commission on Integrated Long-Term Strategy stated that:

> Security assistance is the most important means to preserve free peoples against violence that could imperil a fledgling democracy (as in El Salvador), increase pressures for large-scale migration to the United States (as in Central American wars), jeopardize important American bases (as in the Philippines), threaten vital sea lanes (as in the Persian Gulf), or provide strategic opportunities for the Soviet Union and its proxies.[37]

The only way this important tool can be properly managed, and the only way it can compete with other national security programs, is through the good offices of the NSC Staff in its role as the broker of the national security strategy of the United States.

Industry

In his farewell address in 1961, President Eisenhower warned of the growing impact of what he called the "military-industrial complex." This expression has often been used, in a quasi-Marxist fashion, as a synonym for evil incarnate within American society. But what Eisenhower actually had in mind was not so much an insidious conspiracy of malevolent capitalists and deranged generals, as popular literature would have us believe. Rather, his "military-industrial complex" actually refers to well-meaning, talented people unfortunately operating from dramatically different frames of reference—a confluence of the U.S. Armed Forces, the defense industry, science, education, and government. But, although not perhaps intentionally malignant, this interrelationship between government and the private sector has evolved into a pervasive element of our national security and has created important strategic inconsistencies. As Nick Kotz, writing on the tortured history of the B-1 bomber, has said: "The story of those politics (of the B-1) reveals how national-defense programs have been buffeted back and forth over the years—not only by an evolving Soviet threat, but also

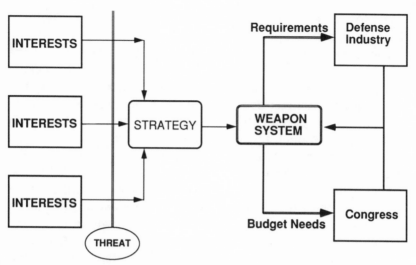

FIGURE 4.3 The procurement maelstrom

by myriad special interests competing in the political and economic maelstrom of American democracy."[38]

This competition often has little to do with a national security
blueprint or strategic requirements. Instead, we find Congressmen
supporting constituents, industry protecting investors, and presidents keeping promises. There is often a serious lack of strategic
rationale behind their decisions, and indeed, major procurement
decisions with national security implications are often in direct
conflict with the actual requirements derived from threats to
global interests. The national security system then needs to
reconcile the demands being placed on it from several directions
(see Figure 4.3).

In a pristine world, we would expect an orderly analytical
and programmatic flow—from the identification of interests
worldwide, through an analysis of the threats to those interests,
to selection of interrelated strategies to control those threats.
These strategies, in turn, would be operationalized into specific
resource requirements, some of which would be weapons systems.
In truth, the system often finds itself locked in Kotz's maelstrom
of competing demands having little to do with national security

needs. As inelegant as that reality is, it must be integrated into the overall national security calculus.

The defense industry places considerable pressure on the national security system, largely because of its need to make a profit. In a capitalist economy, this is neither surprising nor unhealthy. The danger occurs when the national security system is unable to cope with these pressures or reconcile them with overarching national security needs. But reconciliation is not simply a matter of filtering out the lobbyists or ignoring the pressure from industry.

The national security of the United States is inextricably intertwined with the health of its defense industries, the status of which is often determined by specific weapons procurement decisions. As Frank Carlucci, in his final report to the Congress, said, "our strategy of deterrence and ultimately our national security depend upon the continued productive capacity of our industrial base."[39] With this perspective, there may be times when it is prudent to buy a weapons system from a beleaguered defense industry when there appears to be no threat-based requirement for it or when another company could do as well in producing the system. In choosing the contractor to build the B-1, for example, Deputy Secretary of Defense David Packard was heavily influenced by the dire economic straits in which Rockwell International found itself at the time. After Rockwell was awarded the contract, CEO Willard Rockwell said "we knew as a company we had one more chance."[40] This somewhat cumbersome form of government subsidy may be needed in order to keep a company alive and as a hedge against a demand in the future for national mobilization.

Over the long haul, it makes economic sense to diversify the defense industry so that it can produce profitably without sole reliance on defense contracts. For the immediate future, however, Kotz was probably correct when he argued that "defense spending has become a narcotic, and the country is hooked."[41]

The integration of defense industry considerations into the national security equation is not just a matter of sensible weapons acquisition decisions. It requires a more comprehensive examination of the defense industry as a whole in order to arrest what Carlucci has described as the "erosion of this critical defense foundation."[42] The Packard Commission, tasked by the DoD to examine this issue, proposed six major recommendations, most of which underscore the need for the military-industrial complex, including its congressional component, to engage in cooperative reform. As with other factors, this issue demonstrates anew the need for transdepartmental coordination and a new sensitivity to the widening reach of national security.

Congress

Edwin Corwin once said that "The United States Constitution is an invitation to the President and to the Congress to struggle for the privilege of conducting American foreign policy."[43] Since the Vietnam war, that struggle has moved to the fore in the conduct of not only foreign policy but national security policy as a whole. Whether the president or the Congress is winning the struggle depends upon one's perspective; Brzezinski argued that "Congress has become . . . more central in the shaping of national security policy."[44] Professors Rourke and Farnen, on the other hand, asserted that "Congress has been thoroughly vanquished," at least as far as the struggle over the authority to commit U.S. forces to combat.[45]

Views of the relative power of the president and the Congress in national security affairs are largely matters of perception and nuance. What is clear, however, is that Congress will no longer sit by passively and follow the lead of the president. Congressman Lee Hamilton, for one, promised that "the assertiveness and activism of the Congress . . . is going to continue."[46]

This creates some important challenges within the national security system in the executive branch, for the Congress can be shortsighted, ambiguous, slow, and amateurish when dealing with complex issues of international relations.[47] Congress's role has been largely that of nay-sayer, acting as a check on presidential excesses; the Congress has rarely developed innovative policy itself. The few times congressional leaders have tried to take the lead—the efforts of Jim Wright in Nicaragua or Richard Lugar in the Philippines, for example—have generally been viewed as failures or embarrassments to the United States.

Although Congress only has a marginal role in developing policy, its power in shaping or negating policy is significant indeed. Two regional examples serve to illustrate this power: arms sales to the Middle East, and U.S. policy toward the Contras.

The Middle East. Congress's ability to veto major arms sales has been used with great impact on the sale of weapons to U.S. allies in the Middle East. The 1981 AWACS deal with Saudi Arabia, which made good sense in terms of protecting vital U.S. interests in the Persian Gulf, was almost derailed by a joint resolution of disapproval in Congress. The ultimate defeat of the resolution in the Senate required the expenditure of enormous political capital and intense personal lobbying by Ronald Reagan. And, approval of the sale notwithstanding, the political storm it created demonstrated to moderate Arab regimes that the United States was not a dependable ally when it came to meeting what they saw as their legitimate security requirements. Subsequent squabbles over further arms sales have driven Saudi Arabia and Kuwait to purchase weapons from other sources, with a concomitant loss to the United States of political influence and economic benefit. Equally disconcerting, the AWACS issue demonstrated that the executive branch, led by the NSC Staff, was unprepared to deal with Congress in an effective manner before the issue became a governmental crisis demanding direct presidential intervention.

The Contras. The tenuous and unpredictable nature of U.S. policy toward Nicaragua and the Contras was a direct reflection of the struggle for national security dominance between the president and the Congress. As with arms sales to the Middle East, Congress's flip-flops on support to the Contras called U.S. reliability into question. More seriously, the issue showed the inability of the United States to follow a consistent and predictable course in national security affairs and implied that the president could not truly speak for the country. As an incidental by-product of this debacle, the Iran-Contra affair was driven, in the first instance, by the Boland Amendments, which prohibited various kinds of support to the Contras, and by the attitude described by David Gergen: "People . . . simply do not trust the Congress with sensitive and covert programs."[48] Throughout the 1980s, including the very end of the Carter administration, the executive and legislative branches were at loggerheads over Central America—an impasse driven largely by the absence of national consensus on proper U.S. strategy toward the region. Only George Bush's modest success in forging an agreement on humanitarian aid to the Contras in the first months of his administration interrupted an unbroken string of congressional-presidential confrontations over who would control national security policy in Central America.

Congress's involvement in national security affairs is certainly not limited to foreign policy. Through the power of the purse and burgeoning congressional staffs looking for causes, Congress has become increasingly involved in shaping U.S. defense policy and strategy and, as an almost unintended byproduct, in dictating the defense component of our national security strategy. Early in the Bush administration, the president announced his decision on modernizing the land-based component of the U.S. nuclear arsenal—50 MX missiles on rail cars and a commitment to deploy small ICBMs (Midgetman) later on. This was not the option of choice for the Defense Department, nor could a persuasive case be made for the option either economically or strategically. The president's selection was based principally on pressures being exerted on the executive branch from the Congress; certain congressional leaders had become enamored with the Midgetman and threatened to hold the entire modernization program hostage to funding of the small missile.

In its role as a charter member of the military-industrial complex, the Congress is also fertile ground for the seeds of programs sown by eager constituents and defense industries. Congress is also the last resort for disgruntled DoD officials seeking to circumvent decisions made by the president. Presidents cannot expect to have much control over groups from the private sector, and Congress is institutionally bound to consider their proposals. However, the efforts of members of the executive branch, some of whom are in uniform, to undermine the president presents a more insidious challenge to orderly national security decision-making. Nick Kotz asserted that: "The military has a responsibility to provide its candid advice to Congress, even when its views differ from those of the President or the Secretary

of Defense. But offering a respectful dissenting military opinion
has too often been followed by an endless aggressive campaign
to reverse the presidential decision."[49]

Presidents have historically been reluctant to discipline their
own subordinates, particularly those in the armed forces, when
end runs are exposed, and this reluctance encourages such
practices throughout the government. Congress willingly and
eagerly abets, and sometimes foments, this sort of behavior.

The struggle between the executive and legislative branches,
as painful and perplexing as it may be, cannot be wished away
or ignored. At best, a modus vivendi can be worked out so
that the struggle does not become excessively dysfunctional.
The executive branch must take the lead in developing a more
effective working relationship with Congress in national security
matters. As Brzezinski pointed out: "We can no longer shape
national strategy or deal with strategic questions simply by
relying on the decision of a President, his national security
adviser, and his secretaries of state and defense. We are no
longer living in an age . . . when foreign policy is the exclusive
prerogative of the executive branch."[50]

The system must account for the reality of congressional
involvement in the business of national security. Virtually all
analysts agree that the key is genuine consultation, not just on
individual decisions but also on overall strategies and policies.
George Bush enjoyed great bipartisan support for his response
to the Panamanian election fraud of 1989 largely because he
worked with the Congress before he decided to send additional
combat power into the Canal Zone. This sort of consultation,
as distasteful and cumbersome as it may appear to many in
the executive branch, will be critical to the development and
execution of national security policy in the future. The national
security system, led by the NSC Staff, must have formal mechanisms for allowing the legislative branch access to the deliberations that lead to policy decisions. This process may involve,
as Brzezinski has proposed, inclusion of key members of Congress
in meetings of the National Security Council, with care taken
to avoid separation-of-powers issues.[51] Another proposal would
establish a Military Action Council, a joint executive-legislative
body that would advise the president on proposed operations

involving military forces.[52] Whatever the form, a compelling case can be made for the formal inclusion of Congress in the deliberative process.

It is evident that the role of the domestic environment in the formulation and execution of national security affairs will become more and more important. The national security system finds itself assailed from all directions. A system that, in theory, should be responsive primarily to the threats to the nation is instead subjected to domestic pressures only marginally related to national security. Even more challenging are domestic considerations that seem to undermine national security, as the Boland Amendments were perceived by Oliver North. As problematic as these influences may be, if the national security structure fails to accommodate them or does not anticipate them in advance, it will find itself being buffeted about by conflicting and powerful forces and will be unable to provide the strategic direction essential to making cohesive and meaningful national security policy.

A Case in Point: Arms Control

Perhaps no issue in contemporary national security demonstrates these complex factors more clearly than arms control. In an ideal state, arms control would be but one element of national security. Ronald Reagan once described arms control as "One of several tools to enhance our national security. Our arms reductions objectives are fully integrated with our national security policies to enhance deterrence, reduce risk, support alliance relationships, and ensure the Soviets do not gain significant unilateral advantage."[53]

Given this straightforward and sensible set of objectives for arms control, it would appear that U.S. negotiating positions should be relatively clear-cut. Even a cursory examination of specific arms control issues, however, demonstrates the complexity that arises in practice. Taking the objectives stated above as a point of departure, we can use the case of the Strategic Arms Reduction Talks (START) to illustrate this point.

Explicit Factors

The arms control objectives specified by Ronald Reagan in themselves lead to contradictory conclusions, and these contradictions demonstrate the sorts of integration problems that the NSC will have to resolve in the future.

1. *Enhance Deterrence.* Perhaps the easiest issue to frame in the START equation is the question of how to use an agreement on strategic weapons to enhance deterrence. Assuming that, as Carlucci has argued, "our goals are deep, equitable, stabilizing and effectively verifiable reductions in . . . strategic offensive arms," the question becomes: What mix of strategic nuclear forces best contributes to deterrence?[54]

Early in the Reagan administration, most of the arms control community argued that deterrence is best enhanced when each side has a survivable capability to inflict unacceptable damage upon the other, even after a first strike has been absorbed.[55] Since it was widely thought that the best way to improve ICBM survivability in the 1980s and 1990s was to increase the target array by deploying mobile launchers, this position argued for emphasis on reductions in warheads but not necessarily launchers. Using this approach, limiting the heavily MIRVed missiles, such as the U.S. Peacekeeper and the Soviet SS-18, should have been the primary objective of the negotiations.

2. *Reduce Risk.* This second objective is, in many ways, the obverse of the first. Deterrence is best supported when both sides share the risk; a reduction of risk for either side may reduce deterrence, at least in matters nuclear. This conflict between the maintenance of deterrence and the reduction of risk was a source of great interagency debate during the framing of START. The position argued by the JCS and supported by the State Department on this question was that risk is reduced when the United States clearly has the ability to execute its nuclear targeting strategy as dictated by the Single Integrated Operations Plan (SIOP).[56] In the context of arms control, this argued for significant reductions in strategic launchers that would, in turn, reduce the number of targets the JCS would have to engage in a nuclear war. Using this approach, the negotiators

should attempt to limit mobile, single-shot missiles, such as the U.S Midgetman and the Soviet SS-24.

Without commenting on the relative merits of these two arguments, it is obvious that the two represented opposite perspectives on the question of the U.S. negotiating position. Predictably, the issue could not be resolved within the departments; it ultimately required the NSC Staff to fashion a compromise and the president to make a final decision.

3. *Support Alliance Relationships.* The issue of START grows even more complicated when the positions of the allies are considered. Rhetoric notwithstanding, U.S. allies in Europe and, to a lesser extent, in Japan, look with great concern on any bilateral negotiations between the superpowers that lowers the nuclear capabilities of the United States. U.S. allies have long recognized that their security is intimately tied to the nuclear capability of the United States and that any change in the nuclear balance between the superpowers can have deleterious effects upon their own security. As Henry Kissinger has said, the ideal war, from a European perspective, is one fought over the heads of the Europeans solely between the United States and the Soviet Union.[57] The horror with which the Europeans greeted the pronouncements at Reykjavik that promised a complete elimination of all nuclear weapons demonstrated the sensitivity of U.S. allies to the removal of nuclear protection.[58]

The question then becomes not one of the nature of the reductions but of their magnitude. Although perhaps overly simplistic, it is reasonably safe to say that the larger the reductions, the greater the concern will be on the part of U.S. allies. Moreover, the concern is not solely with soothing worried allies but rather with the impact of a START agreement on the U.S. alliance structure itself. If the allies feel that the United States is reducing the threat to its own security at the expense of the nuclear umbrella, they will have less confidence in the United States as a reliable partner and will be less inclined to cooperate on other security and economic issues. If one of our arms control objectives is to insure alliance solidarity, START must be carefully crafted to assuage alliance concerns and to insure that these concerns do not have an adverse impact on other spheres of security cooperation.

4. *Insure No Unilateral Soviet Advantage.* In the context of START, this objective not only requires balanced reductions but also capable verification regimes. Assuming that the United States would never allow a unilateral Soviet advantage in the agreement itself that is not offset by some unilateral U.S. advantage, cheating becomes the only way the Soviet Union could achieve such advantages. Effective verification thus becomes the sine qua non for achieving this fourth objective.

Yet verification is clearly the most difficult aspect of arms control in the 1990s. Quite apart from the awesome problems associated with negotiating a verification agreement, there are associated issues that cross into other important national security areas. Two of these, as we have learned from the INF agreement, are intrusion and cost.

Because of the precedent set by the INF agreement and the overarching concern with negotiating air-tight strategic weapons accords, we may assume that a START agreement will contain verification regimes at least as stringent as those in the INF. This, in turn, implies a much larger Soviet presence in the United States, with all the concomitant opportunities for expanded espionage that such a presence affords. Even more problematic is the question of cost. If we extrapolate from the INF On-Site Inspection Agency model and assume that additional satellite assets will be required for verification, costs for a START agreement could run as high as $50 billion. At the extreme, it could prove less expensive to have an arms race than arms control. Although it is unlikely that a START agreement would be derailed over costs alone, these are important factors that will have to be traded off against other national security budget items. Costs, for example, could force a choice between a comprehensive START agreement and the complete modernization of the strategic nuclear arsenal. It is doubtful that the United States could afford both.

Implicit Factors

In addition to the explicit factors described by Reagan's guidelines, there are a number of other pressures that play important roles in shaping the START process. Among these are: public opinion, presidential politics, industrial concerns, Congress, and developments inside the Soviet Union. A brief examination of these factors demonstrates anew the ever-widening national security net cast by arms control.

1. *Public Opinion.* There has historically been a deep and abiding suspicion and fear of nuclear weapons within the United States. This attitude has been manifest not just in the various antinuclear movements that have been more or less powerful across the decades of the nuclear age but also in the view of Americans in the political mainstream. It has translated into the widely held opinion that arms control and arms races are on opposite sides of the same normative coin; arms control is inherently good, and arms races are fundamentally bad. Whatever the particulars of a START proposal may be, no elected official can afford to ignore this basic strain within the American body politic. Arms control has assumed a political momentum all its own and, absent some cataclysmic event in the world, the public expects and demands that the process continue.

2. *Presidential Politics.* As the sole U.S. political leader with a national constituency, the president must be particularly sensitive to the strain of antinuclear pacifism within the American public. This is especially true in the waning months of an election year when his next term is at stake. As concerned as they are with reelection, however, most presidents are even more attuned to their image in history; all presidents want to be remembered as peacemakers and, in the latter decades of the twentieth century, peace equates with arms control. In this regard, it seems no accident that Ronald Reagan became the great arms controller only in his second term. These concerns, coupled with Mikhail Gorbachev's public diplomacy offensive, created significant pressure on George Bush to reach a START agreement in his first term. On a smaller scale, these pressures certainly contributed in a major way to President Bush's May 1989 initiative on conventional arms control.[59]

These pressures are unique to the president and are not routinely considered as part of the arms control equation by the departments. Yet, these are important considerations and will have a role in the formulation and pace of a START agreement.

3. *Industry.* The defense industry is remarkably well informed on the START process and on proposals being considered within the national security structure. Defense contractors see both risks and opportunities embedded in any START agreement. The risks are obvious; a contractor could easily see a multibillion dollar business venture evaporate because of an agreement that eliminates the system being produced. Bomber counting rules, for example, could well limit the size of the strategic bomber fleet and could endanger Northrop's B-2 production contracts. At the same time, verification requirements are creating a new growth industry, and defense contractors are eager to jump aboard with high dollar proposals.

In either case, it is clear that defense industry leaders can play an active role in formulating negotiating positions and determining the ultimate acceptability of an agreement. The avenues by which they make their views known can be circuitous indeed, but the pressure they can exert cannot be ignored.

Moreover, if we accept the premise that the health of the defense industry is an integral part of our national security, then protection of the industrial base is an appropriate and necessary consideration in any arms control agreement. It may be, to use the B-2 example cited above, that START bomber counting rules should be adjusted to allow the production of some number of B-2s, if it is determined that such a run is necessary to sustain Northrop's economic health.

The effective integration of industry's concerns into the START process is a complex requirement that goes far beyond the arms control structure as routinely configured. This factor again underscores the need for a new and imaginative structural approach to the management of arms control in particular and national security in general.

4. *Congress.* Congress's role in the arms control process is vital. For the past two decades, the Senate has seen itself as the court of last resort in insuring that arms control agreements adequately protect national security. As the Limited Test Ban Treaty and SALT II have demonstrated, congressional support of arms control agreements cannot be assumed. The Senate is particularly sensitive to the issue of verification and, since the

Senate plays a prominent role in the treaty process, it is important to involve key senators early in the deliberations.

Although, as in the case of both treaties mentioned, it is possible for a president to adhere to the terms of an unratified treaty, the requirement for Congress to fund the START verification regimes cannot be avoided. This factor will play an especially prominent role in START, as it appears that verification will involve major expenditures. Therefore, both houses of Congress must be involved in the process early on. It would be a major setback for the United States if a START agreement was not ratified by the Senate or not funded by the House. In order to avoid a Versailles Treaty debacle, the arms control community must fully integrate congressional concerns during the negotiations.

Congressional loyalty to local constituents is another part of the equation. Arms control agreements prior to START largely focused on controlling new production and growth or on esoteric systems that had little impact on local economies. In START, however, major reductions in strategic forces are contemplated, reductions that could take ICBM wings out of the inventory, force a drawdown on manned bomber squadrons, and reduce the fleet of ballistic missile submarines. The loss of these units, and the payrolls they provide, will have an important impact on local economies. Congress, in turn, could respond by trying to protect local interests by preserving certain strategic systems based solely on the role these systems play in supporting local economies. Although arms control has to date not been largely influenced by this kind of pressure from Congress, that could well change in the context of START.

5. *The Soviet Union.* Any arms control agreement, no matter how sophisticated its verification regimes, must be based on a certain amount of mutual trust. In this regard, the composition and attitude of the government of the Soviet Union will obviously play a prominent role in the future of START. In the early 1990s, it appears that both superpowers are genuinely interested in concluding a strategic arms reduction agreement, and this interest creates an atmosphere that allows far greater flexibility in the negotiations themselves than did, say, the atmosphere prevailing during the early Carter years, when the Soviet Union

had no interest in reductions. Clearly, the change in Soviet leadership and the economic morass in which the Soviet Union finds itself have created a far more receptive climate for arms control than existed in the not-too-distant past.

More than any other arms control agreement, START will be based upon, and hostage to, continued benign behavior on the part of the Soviet Union. In this regard, Gorbachev is now the prisoner of his own success; he has received much good press because he has softened his country's well-deserved reputation as an international bully. But, by changing that image, Gorbachev has established a different set of standards by which the Soviet Union will be measured. The Soviet invasion of Czechoslovakia in 1968 and thinly veiled Soviet threats against Poland in 1981 barely caused yawns in the international community because of the widely held expectations of villainous Soviet behavior. The Soviet Union of the 1990s faces a far different set of international expectations; a Soviet invasion of an East European country or a crackdown in one of its republics in the future would cause far greater damage to the international reputation of the Soviet Union than it ever would have in the past. It is somewhat ironic that the long-standing Soviet position of opposing linkage between arms control and international behavior has been most effectively destroyed by Gorbachev's own public relations success.

The sensitivity of START to future Soviet behavior is reinforced by the nature of the weapons under negotiation. For the first time, the United States is staking some measure of its own survival on an arms control agreement with its most ardent adversary. Any hint of neo-Stalinism or even a plateau in the headlong rush of the Soviet Union to responsible international behavior can be expected to have significant implications for the future of START.

Arms Control as a Microcosm

The future of arms control, and especially START, is dependent upon a complex range of influences that goes far beyond the issues explicitly identified by the articulated national security strategy of the United States. These influences are schematically presented in Figure 4.4.

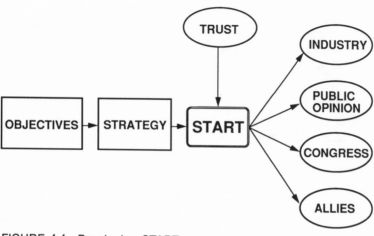

FIGURE 4.4   Developing START

Arms control negotiators can no longer consider proposals in the pristine environment of technical detail; if an agreement of any type, particularly one involving central systems, is to reach fruition, it must take into account the expanding range of concerns and participants involved in the arms control business. As in so many other areas, the NSC Staff must take the lead in this process to insure that the widest possible net is cast in the development of negotiating positions.

But the Staff's record is not admirable in this regard, as amply demonstrated during the early Reagan years. At a time when no consensus existed within the government on even the theoretical utility of arms control, the NSC Staff allowed competing views to grow into dysfunctional schisms; without a powerful NSC Staff, no effective policy could emerge. As START student Strobe Talbott said, "The NSC Staff . . . tried to arbitrate, reconcile, synthesize. The result was not so much synthesis as paralysis."[60] Carnes Lord, a member of the Staff at the time, agreed with this assessment, saying that NSC Staff ineptitude "led to a situation marked by paralysis of normal interagency procedures and spasmodic and ad hoc decision-making at the top."[61] The Staff was simply unable to come to grips with the myriad considerations, interests, and perspectives flowing around arms control.

Although lessons come hard, they can be learned; the arms control community of the late Reagan and early Bush administrations demonstrate that organizational progress can be made. Both structures placed the White House, led by the NSC Staff, firmly in control of the entire arms control process. This does not necessarily mean that arms control was immediately rationalized across the entire spectrum of the national security structure. It did mean, however, that the possibility for such organizational reconciliation now existed.

Conclusion

The national security system of the United States was originally constructed to respond to changes in the international system wrought by the Second World War and the development of a bipolar world. As dramatic as those changes were, they pale in comparison to the revolution in the international order taking place in the 1990s. The environment in which the national security of the United States is embedded grows almost daily in complexity, both internationally and domestically. If the United States is to protect its national security effectively, the national security system must be redesigned so that decisions and policies reflect the expanding scope of the discipline. This will involve, in the first instance, a new look at the structure of the National Security Council and its supporting Staff. In the twenty-first century the United States will no longer be able to afford the luxury of managing national security with a structural-functional mismatch growing out of a system beset with patchwork solutions and built from an archaic design.

5

A Prescription for the Future

It is evident that different presidents have created different national security structures with differing degrees of success. Most analysts agree with the Tower Commission's assertion that "the [national security] system is properly the President's creature. It must be left flexible to be molded by the President into the form most useful to him."[1] The president's relationship to his top national security advisers and the various bureaucracies they lead will be shaped, to some extent, by his personality, his experiences, and his management style. It will also be shaped by the personalities and abilities of the principal participants in the national security process.

At the same time, the president's freedom to shape his national security structure and his chances of seeing it endure beyond the first year of his administration are severely constrained by the pressures of national security itself. It appears that inexorable forces emanating from the international and domestic environments are increasingly driving modern presidents into more intimate involvement in national security affairs and propelling the executive branch into Brzezinski's presidential system of decision-making. Whatever the president's preferences may be, centralized management of national security affairs will be mandated by the future. No longer will it be realistic for a president to choose a management system centered on the State Department; national security has outgrown the narrow confines of foreign policy and must be considered a new and overarching management discipline that needs an effective supporting structure. Although a president can, and probably should, make his secretary of state his foreign policy spokesperson, that is but a single slice of the national security pie. The secretary of state should be the first among equals, but equal only in a conceptual second tier of the national security process.

Within this context, it now appears that there are, indeed, functional requisites that must be performed if the national security system is to work. Given these two factors, and with the caveat that no two presidents will structure the system identically, there should be basic similarities in how different administrations answer three fundamental quesitons: (1) What should the APNSA do? (2) How should the NSC Staff be configured? and (3) How should Staff responsibilities be articulated? In this chapter, we will attempt to construct answers to these questions and, as a result, create a prototype for the future.

The Role of the Assistant
to the President

Although the thrust of this discussion has been the NSC Staff, we must examine the role of the APNSA in order to present a meaningful position on the Staff itself. More than any other organization in the national security system, the NSC Staff is the product of its principal—in this case, the APNSA— and it is his role that will ultimately determine the Staff's ability to execute its requisite functions.

As distasteful as it may be to many in the national security business, the assistant to the president for national security affairs must be one of the three primary actors in national security. Leslie Gelb has argued that the system cannot "turn the prince back into a frog" and cannot return the APNSA to what some see as his ideal role—the Bundy or the Cutler model.[2] The chaos of the Reagan NSC was due, in large measure, to the efforts of Meese and Haig to turn the clock back to a system now rendered irrelevant by the evolving demands of national security. Instead, the basic document organizing the national security system of the future should recognize and facilitate the modern role of the APNSA. As Odeen said, "There has been a fundamental change in the nature of the problems over the past fifteen or twenty years that has tended to give the national security adviser a much heavier role, a much more public role, and a much more important role."[3]

As we have seen, the APNSA must effectively function in two sometimes conflicting capacities. First, he must function as the manager of the national security system, wearing the hat of the assistant to the president for national security affairs. Second, he must act as the personal counselor to the president on national security matters in his capacity as the national security adviser. If the APNSA/NSA is deficient in either capacity or if the structure creates insurmountable obstacles along either path, then the entire national security system will not work.

In his first role, the APNSA must oversee the NSC and its supporting Staff objectively. He must insure that the Staff executes the requisite functions in an effective and judicious manner. As the Tower Commission asserted:

> It is his responsibility to ensure that matters submitted for consideration by the Council cover the full range of issues on which review is required; that those issues are fully analyzed; that a full range of options is considered; that the prospects and risks of each are examined; that all relevant intelligence and other information is available to the principals; that difficulties in implementation are confronted.[4]

In this capacity, he serves primarily the institution of the National Security Council and, although perhaps not as invisible as Sidney Souers's "anonymous servant," he should be an honest, noncontroversial broker of the system. His neutrality on issues, however, should not be confused with passivity; he may indeed be very assertive in what Odeen calls "decision forcing" and in policy supervision.[5] The APNSA will have to crack the whip to make the national security system work, to forge consensus, to insure that the bureaucracy is presenting issues fairly and imaginatively, and to demand adherence to the president's decisions.

At the same time, the NSA must serve as a personal adviser to the president. The Tower Commission reached the conclusion that "he is perhaps the one most able to see things from the President's perspective . . . [and] is unburdened by departmental responsibilities."[6] Former Secretary of Defense Harold Brown, the beneficiary and the victim of a strong NSA, has contended that "the NSC Advisor must do more than coordinate—he must represent the President's views."[7] It is both unrealistic and dangerous to argue, as Haig did, that the "National Security Adviser should be a staff man—not a maker of policy."[8] It is equally damaging to support I. M. Destler's view that the position should be abolished altogether.[9] The nature of national security and the environmental challenges facing any president in the future simply will not allow the luxury of returning to the past. The APNSA and the Staff he leads have become necessary fixtures on the national security scene; the organizational challenge is to make the most out of this reality.

Many critics of the NSA argue his role based primarily on his public posture, sometimes measuring his performance by the number of times his name appears in print.[10] Although this line of criticism becomes more emotional than real, it highlights the entire question of public posture—an issue that must be decided by the president. In the execution of the functional requisites, it is not essential that the NSA be a public spokesman, but if he is, then the administration needs to insure that the NSA and the other public figures in the government are espousing a coherent and consistent national security policy line.

Being a public spokesman, however, is not an essential part of the position itself. The national security system must recognize that the elevation of the NSA has been brought about, not as a by-product of strong egos and personalities, but by the demands of an increasingly complex international environment. For all its weaknesses, the Carter administration recognized this reality and produced notable successes in national security. For all its strengths, the Reagan administration did not, and the result was an unnecessarily chaotic and directionless national security system. Ever the journalist, Leslie Gelb summarized the issue neatly in his two "iron laws." The first point, Gelb argued, is that "things won't work well with a strong national security adviser to the President. The second is that, without a strong adviser, things won't work at all."[11]

How, then, should an administration structure the national security system to facilitate the dual roles of the APNSA/NSA? Brzezinski, R. D. MacLaurin, and others have proposed that the status of the APNSA be upgraded to formal cabinet level, either as the director or the secretary of national security, possibly even subject to Senate confirmation.[12] These dramatic proposals would certainly resolve the internecine squabbling that seems endemic in each administration and would position the incumbent to fulfill both of his primary roles. Moreover, the establishment of a Department of National Security would put managerial substance to the multifaceted nature of national security.

But this proposal, however attractive from a functional perspective, has several important drawbacks. First, it is probably not feasible; the establishment of a Department of National Security would surely elicit a storm of protests, opposition, and cabinet-level resignations if it were seriously considered. Congress has long been comfortable with the illusion that the secretary of state manages national security and, given that institution's conservative nature when it comes to major reorganization, would present possibly insurmountable obstacles. Second, even if such a department were established, it would require that the new secretary be confirmed by the Senate. Although some, including Brzezinski, have argued that this would not be all that bad, it would undermine the freedom and confidentiality with which the APNSA currently operates. As a result, he could become a less effective confidant of the president, and this, in turn, would generate incentive for the president to create another advisory post not subject to Senate confirmation. Third, the establishment of a department would create the very sorts of bureaucratic inertia that the NSC Staff is best in avoiding. It would do little good to establish an organization that, by the very fact of its establishment, undermined a substantial part of its raison d'être.

Short of establishing a Department of National Security, another approach would be to modify the current national security structure, spelling out in detail the specific roles of the

APNSA and then giving him the bureaucratic leverage he needs to execute them. At a minimum, the APNSA should chair the important sub-NSC committees in which much of the business of national security is conducted. The NSC Staff should then chair the committees subordinate to those chaired by the APNSA, in recognition of the validity of Haig's pronouncement that "he who controls the key IGs . . . controls policy."[13]

In addition, the APNSA should be explicitly assigned the crisis management portfolio and the ability to task throughout the government in the execution of his crisis management role. The APNSA must also be afforded unfettered access to the president with no intervening layers in the White House. Finally, he must be afforded clear cabinet status and be recognized as coequal with the secretaries of state and defense. These recommendations run against the grain of many NSC critics, but their implementation is essential if the United States is to return to an effective national security system.

One issue separating the critics from the proponents of a strong NSA concerns the high standards of personal qualities that would be required. Critics argue that, although it would be nice if one person could effectively act in the dual roles demanded of the position, no such person can be found. Supporters contend that, although the population of such people is small, it does exist and can be drawn upon. Qualities necessary for success as the APNSA/NSA include the following:

1. *Competence.* The APNSA must be conversant in the entire range of national security issues or, at least, must know where his weaknesses are and act to redress them.

2. *Experience.* The APNSA cannot come into the position as a novice to government. He must not only understand the formal structure of the bureaucracy but must also be familiar with the entrenched issues and individuals. He must understand how and when to pull the right levers to make the system work.

3. *Intellect.* He must be both pragmatic and conceptual, able to generate ideas and then translate them into meaningful policy. Moreover, he must have an established intellectual reputation in order to command instant respect in the government, in the academic world, in the Congress, and in the media. He must

be an intellectual magnet that can attract the brightest and most innovative people into the NSC Staff. Carnes Lord argued forcefully that "the NSC has been at its strongest and most independent under advisers who had an academic base," and proposed that the APNSA be chosen from the academic world as a matter of course.[14] Although this view is perhaps extreme, it does underscore the importance of a commanding intellect as an important characteristic for an effective APNSA.

4. *Ethics.* The APNSA must have a sufficiently strong ethical foundation to be able to act as an honest broker in coordinating and integrating the national security system. As Walt Rostow said, "he must be able to present another man's case as well as the man himself could."[15] The entire national security system must have confidence that the APNSA will present alternate views fairly and will not take advantage of propinquity in the coordination of papers and positions. He must be able to present bad news to the president and to sniff out and squelch misbehavior before it becomes a problem. He must be scrupulously honest in presenting presidential decisions and in monitoring the implementation process. Perhaps most important, he must impart the same sense of ethical behavior to the Staff he leads.

5. *Loyalty.* If he is to function as a personal adviser to the president, the NSA must believe in the man he serves. He must consider that his first duty is to support the president while insuring that he never overshadows or upstages his boss. He must elicit the trust and confidence of the president in order to act effectively in his stead within the national security system.

6. *Tact.* The APNSA will, by the very nature of his position, elicit envy and animosity from the departments. He must make a concerted and continuous effort to salve wounded egos, maintain cordial relations with abrasive personalities throughout the government, and present triumphs and defeats in a manner that helps smooth the way for cooperation on the next issue.

7. *Confidence.* He must be confident in his own abilities and in those of his staff in order to hold his own in the tumult of conflicting opinions that marks any national security system.

A final quality is that the APNSA/NSA should be a civilian. A military officer, although certainly capable of possessing all of the traits listed above, operates from two perceptual disadvantages. First, military officers are unfairly seen to possess only modest intellectual capabilities. This makes it especially difficult for an officer to be taken seriously in the formulation and advocacy of policy. Carnes Lord asserted, "There is little reason to expect that general officers in the US Armed Forces will have acquired a solid grounding in higher strategic studies or in political-military affairs."[16] This view, although not reflective of the current generation of military leaders, is widely held and leads to a certain intellectual condescension toward the uniformed services.

Second, there remains within the government a psychohistorical suspicion of a strong military role in the development of policy. Many Americans are simply uncomfortable with an officer crossing the line between policy execution and policy formulation. For these reasons, the position of APNSA/NSA is better filled with a civilian.

Although this is a daunting list of qualities, there are certainly those in government, in academia, and in the private sector who meet all of them. These should form the population from which the APNSA/NSA is drawn.

The National Security Council Staff

The NSC Staff must be supported by a national security structure that allows for the smooth execution of the functional requisites. But in addition to the external structure, the size, internal organization, and composition of the Staff itself are key variables in the effectiveness of the entire system.

Size

The NSC Staff has varied greatly in size over the past forty years, ranging from three to more than fifty professionals. In determining the appropriate size, a balance must be struck between efficiency and flexibility; the Staff must be large enough to cover the entire spectrum of national security issues with some degree of expertise. Scowcroft has pointed out that long-range planning is often inadequately done because "the NSC Staff is constrained as to the number of people available. . . . Our limited personnel assets were used to 'put out fires.'"[17]

This argues for a Staff larger than that routinely maintained by the NSC. Indeed, if we consider the range of national security concerns with which the Staff must deal, it becomes clear that it must grow beyond historical levels. The Staff has regularly been accused of being "a mile wide and an inch deep," a criticism of its lack of expertise in specific areas. In reality, the Staff is closer to a foot wide and an inch deep in a mile-wide national security environment. It has largely been unable to keep pace with the expanding scope of national security concerns and to manage an effective integration of the various elements of national power. The size of the Staff should be sufficient to provide knowledgeable leadership in all the functional areas relevant to national security.

At the same time, the Staff must be small enough to avoid the rigidity that marks most large organizations. Larger staffs invite layering, which is useful to a degree, but in the NSC environment it would undermine the flexibility and intimacy essential to effective operation. Moreover, a large Staff would be additional bureaucratic evidence that a rival department had been created in the White House—a perception that would lead to dysfunctional friction. It is not necessary to hire enough Staff members to have expertise matching the departments in all areas; it is breadth, rather than depth, that is important on the NSC Staff. The expertise necessary to make informed decisions is the proper purview of the departments, and it is sufficient that the NSC Staff have access to this wealth of knowledge.

It is difficult to empirically determine an ideal size for the NSC Staff. Although persuasive justification for an exact size probably cannot be offered, it appears that seventy-five to eighty professionals is about the right number. A Staff much smaller than that could not contend with the range of issues that must be considered by the NSC in order to manage national security effectively. A Staff much larger would become a bureaucracy unto itself in which individual Staff members would lack a personal relationship with the APNSA and the president himself.[18]

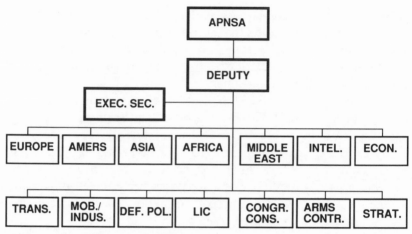

FIGURE 5.1   NSC Staff configuration

Staff Organization

The Tower Commission, reacting to the aberration that was
the Iran-Contra affair, recommended an organization designed
to maximize supervision. "Clear vertical lines of control and
authority, responsibility, and accountability, are essential to good
management."[19] This is a useful point of departure, but caution
must be exercised; such an organization can become excessively
structured and rigid. The designers of the next Staff organization
must not try to remedy the Oliver North phenomenon by
structural solutions; the Iran-Contra affair occurred primarily
because of personality flaws in North and Poindexter rather
than faults within the system itself. Supervision and accountability are necessary but should not come at the expense of
flexibility and intellectual freedom. Staff members must be able
to interact with each other across nominal staff lines, form ad
hoc working groups to deal with specific issues, and draw upon
each other's expertise.

One organization that supports these goals is a three-tiered
system as outlined in Figure 5.1. The first tier, the simplest and
most traditional, is made up of the APNSA, his deputy, and
his executive secretary. Below the first tier, however, the structure
departs significantly from the Staff organizations of the past.
The second layer is composed of the directors of the regional

and functional groups, and in the third layer, we find the Staff officers who execute the basic tasks of managing national security. The term "cluster" was used by the Brzezinski NSC Staff, and it seems to convey the proper mix of informality and structure and so will be used here.

The regional and functional clusters hold the key to the success or failure of the Staff in executing its requisite functions and must be carefully crafted to insure full consideration and integration of the ever-expanding scope of national security considerations. The regional clusters mirror those found in the Department of State and the Department of Defense and, therefore, allow for smoother interdepartmental coordination on regional issues. The functional clusters embrace a wide range of issue areas, some of which are not normally included in the Staff structure. Therefore, they warrant a brief discussion.

1. *Defense Policy.* This cluster would focus on the military instrument of national power and insure that the DoD and the Joint Chiefs of Staff (JCS) were fully integrated into the national security process. The importance of the defense cluster is closely tied to the role of the JCS. Under the provisions of the Goldwater-Nichols Defense Reorganization Act, the chairman of the JCS assumed new responsibilities as the principal military adviser to the president. The role of the defense cluster will change depending on the extent to which the chairman of the JCS is used in that capacity—the stronger the chairman, the less need for a strong defense cluster. In a climate in which the chairman is an active and trusted member of the national security team, the defense cluster would focus most of its energies on its coordination mission and its role in the orchestration of the military component of national strategy. In an atmosphere in which the chairman's advice is not actively sought, the defense cluster would emphasize its advisory and policy formulation roles.

In either case, the defense cluster would provide the White House interface between national security and the defense budget, coordinating the views of the Defense Department and the OMB. The defense cluster would also have special responsibility in providing the White House representative on nuclear issues, to include targeting doctrine, continuity of government, and telecommunications.

2. *Economics.* This cluster would be tasked with the integration of economic issues, both domestic and international, into the national security equation. In this capacity, it would be the primary Staff coordinator with the departments of Treasury and Commerce, as well as with the president's Council of Economic Advisers. The mission of the economics cluster would not be to develop economic policy as much as it would be to insure that economic options and considerations are fully integrated into the NSC process. The economics cluster would also be the primary Staff element to effect dialogue on trade-offs to be made within the various national security budgets. In this role, the cluster would monitor the national security budget, particularly those areas not directly subsumed under defense programs.

3. *Low-Intensity Conflict.* Because LIC transcends traditional bureaucratic boundaries, a separate Staff cluster should be established to deal with the issues it raises. The National Security Council has had LIC responsibilities since its inception, but the Staff mechanisms for executing this task efficiently have been generally absent. LIC embraces a wide range of threats and a wider range of U.S. options. Thus, LIC must not be considered the exclusive domain of the defense establishment; indeed, many LIC threats are not amenable to a U.S. military response. The LIC cluster must take a broad look at the LIC phenomenon and plumb the entire national security establishment to develop effective solutions.

The LIC cluster could assume management of the U.S. security assistance program in order to provide a knowledgeable resource close to the president and insure that security assistance programs are fully considered as an efficacious means to further national security. Part of the eclectic LIC cluster would also deal with international terrorism, often considered an instrument of low-intensity conflict.

4. *Transnational Issues.* This cluster would be responsible for the issues of emerging national security importance that cut across national boundaries. Such concerns as international pollution, the environment, population control, disease, and hunger will clearly present challenges to national security in the future

and must be incorporated into the Staff structure in an effective manner. The transnational cluster would also assume a coordinating role in the War on Drugs.

Perhaps more than any other cluster, the transnational issues group would be in danger of becoming irrelevant to the national security process. Accordingly, great attention must be paid to staffing this group with persons of great energy and credibility.

5. *Mobilization and Industry.* This group would undertake the daunting task of reconciling national security with the needs of domestic industry. Since it is evident that the health of our defense industry is an integral part of our overall national security posture, and since it is equally apparent that defense contractors will play an increasing role in the development of national security policy, the NSC Staff should be structured to account for, and integrate, these concerns into the decisional process.

This cluster would also handle national mobilization, insuring that the widest possible integration is being effected by the relevant agencies and departments in the planning process. The mobilization and industry group would also assume the responsibility for dealing with domestic emergencies, such as major earthquakes, that have national security overtones. As such, this cluster would be the primary White House coordinator for the Federal Emergency Management Agency (FEMA).

6. *Congressional Consultations.* From the discussion presented earlier, it is evident that congressional involvement in the national security system will expand in the future. Accordingly, it is necessary to institutionalize the consultative process so that conflict between the White House and Congress can be minimized. To accomplish this, the National Security Council should be expanded to include the senior leadership from both houses, not during the decisional process but in meetings when options are being presented and discussed.

The responsibilities of this congressional consultations cluster would extend beyond those normally executed by liaison staffs. This cluster would provide full-time support to those key members of Congress regularly included in NSC deliberations. Members of the cluster would serve two masters—the APNSA and the congressional representatives. This approach would help to keep members of Congress involved in the consultative process while avoiding the concomitant involvement of congressional staffs.

7. *Arms Control.* After the experience of the Carter and Reagan administrations, it is almost axiomatic to say that arms control must be run from the White House. The NSC Staff must have the means to force the incorporation of arms control into a cohesive national security strategy and to forge consensus in this most contentious area. Experienced diplomats largely responsive to the Department of State should continue to handle the negotiations themselves, but the NSC Staff should orchestrate policy issues and the general direction of negotiating positions. This cluster would be the single point of institutional contact within the Staff dedicated to the arms control issue.

8. *Intelligence.* The NSC has always had a special relationship with the intelligence community (IC), and this relationship ought to continue in the future. Effective management of the IC and the full and effective integration of intelligence as an element of national power rest with White House oversight. Assigning this responsibility to members of the NSC Staff has proved effective in the past and should be an essential element of any Staff configuration in the future.

9. *National Strategy Planning.* Perhaps most controversial of all, this group would be the focal point for the president's ongoing effort to develop, articulate, and refine the national security strategy of the United States. The establishment of a separate and standing Staff cluster for this purpose would help guarantee that strategic planning was not simply a one-shot effort done at the beginning of each administration and would help insure that all operational and budgetary considerations of national strategy planning are taken into account.

In executing its responsibilities, the NSP group must take care not to stray over the line separating its own responsibilities from those of the departments and agencies. Foreign policy strategy and military strategy must remain, for example, with the departments of State and Defense respectively. But the national security strategy that overarches these separate programs must be generated and coordinated by the NSC Staff.

Obviously, there are a number of ways to structure the Staff to meet its functional requisites in the context of the international and domestic environments of the future. But whatever its ultimate configuration, the Staff organization must be at once flexible and structured. It must be flexible enough to foster horizontal coordination between Staff members and between directors; it must be structured enough to discourage direct, special relationships from developing between the first tier and the Staff members—such as occurred between Poindexter and North.

The position of executive secretary bears special mention. This is the only Staff position specifically authorized in the 1947 legislation, and it can be used to great advantage by the APNSA and the Staff in executing the process functions. The executive secretary can help relieve the APNSA from much of the more mundane, yet critical, process functions, freeing him up to focus more attention on policy substance. The executive secretary position fell into disuse during the Nixon and Ford years but can be a post of great utility.

In the same vein, there is value in establishing a small and relatively permanent policy group within the Staff, in addition to the current nonpolicy secretariat. This group would allow for substantive and administrative continuity between presidencies and would help prevent each administration from having to learn the same lessons that its predecessor struggled to learn.

Staff Composition

It is a relatively simple task to structure the Staff to meet the national security demands of the future, but it is quite another to make it all work. Effective structure is a necessary but not a sufficient condition in the management effort—it is the people who fill the structure who must make it work. In 1961, McGeorge Bundy said, in a letter to Senator Henry Jackson, that the NSC Staff "should be composed of men [sic] equally well versed in the process of planning and in that of operational follow-up."[20] Twenty years later, this is still sound guidance. The members of the NSC Staff should be drawn from the widest range of sources possible: the departments of State and Defense, the Intelligence Community, the Treasury Department, the academic world, and the private sector. They would share the qualities of the APNSA, with emphasis on selflessness and confidence. They must be experienced within the government and well-connected with all relevant departments and agencies.

But they should not stay on the Staff indefinitely. One of the conclusions of the Tower Commission was that members of the Staff should not remain for longer than four years.[21] Rotation of Staff members is the safest way to insure that new ideas and fresh approaches are continuously being introduced into the system. Moreover, and perhaps less idealistically, rotation is the best way to hedge against the folly of individual Staff members who lose touch with their ethical foundations and constitutional idealism. Many members of the Staff have commented on the erosion of ethical values that occurs after the third year on the White House staff and how morally numbing the entire process can become.

Articulation of the Structure

Many administrations, regardless of their individual national security systems, have developed implicit understandings about the roles and missions of the Staff. But no president has outlined his desires for the NSC Staff clearly and with formal presidential blessing. PD-2, for example, says only that "The Assistant to the President shall be assisted by a National Security Council staff, as provided by law."[22] NSDD-2 is silent on the role of the Staff.

In light of all that has been discussed thus far, it is apparent that the responsibilities of the NSC Staff must be explicitly articulated in a presidential directive. This document should be separate from that which lays out the basic national security system and should be clear about what the Staff should and should not do. What follows is a proposed directive document which could serve as a point of departure for any administration in insuring that the structural-functional mismatch within the national security system is minimized.

National Security Directive-3

The National Security Council Staff

In support of the National Security Council System mandated in NSD-2 and in accordance with the National Security Act of 1947, the National Security Council Staff is established.

I. *Functions of the National Security Council Staff.* The NSC Staff shall act in three capacities.

First, it shall serve as the staff of the National Security Council under the direction of the assistant to the president for national security affairs. In that capacity, the Staff shall be responsible for the administration of the NSC system. It shall also be responsible for the coordination and integration of policy in preparation for submission to the NSC for consideration. It shall also be responsible for supervising the implementation of my decisions and for interpreting specific policies.

Second, the Staff shall provide support to the assistant to the president in his capacity as coordinator of crisis management. The NSC Staff shall effect coordination throughout the relevant agencies to insure the presentation of options and the implementation of decisions in a timely manner. It shall convene crisis management working groups subordinate to the NSC and composed of representatives of the involved departments and agencies. It shall also be responsible for crisis contingency planning, drawing upon the departments and agencies for support.

Third, the Staff shall support the assistant to the president in his capacity as the national security adviser. In this regard, the Staff shall be one of my personal staffs and will provide me, through the national security adviser, with recommendations on national security matters.

II. *Organization of the NSC Staff.* The Staff shall be organized into three echelons. At the top shall be the assistant to the president, his deputy, and the executive secretary of the NSC. Next, there shall be fourteen directors chairing groups in the following regional and functional areas: Europe and the Soviet Union, the Middle East and Southwest Asia, Africa, Latin America, the Far East, Intelligence, Economics, Transnational Issues, Defense Policy, Low-Intensity Conflict, Mobilization and Industry, Congressional Consultations, Arms Control, and National Strategy Planning. Third, there shall be Staff officers in each regional and functional group whose work will be supervised by the directors. In addition, there shall be established a Staff Secretariat responsible for administrative support to the NSC and composed of permanent civil servants. It is my intention that the Staff Secretariat provide the administrative continuity between administrations.

III. *Size and Composition of the NSC Staff.* The size of the Staff shall not exceed seventy-five professionals, excluding the assistant to the president, his deputy, the executive secretary, and the Staff Secretariat. The Staff shall be composed of representatives of the Foreign Service, the Armed Forces, the Intelligence Community, the academic community, the private sector, and other sources as required.

IV. *Equivalent Rank of the NSC Staff.* For the purposes of seniority and protocol, the NSC Staff shall have equivalent rank as follows. The assistant to the president shall rank as a member of my cabinet. The deputy assistant to the president shall rank as a deputy secretary. The executive secretary and the group directors shall rank as assistant secretaries. The Staff officers shall rank as deputy assistant secretaries.

V. *Modifications to this Directive.* The assistant to the president may change the composition and structure of the functional and regional groups as required.

This proposed directive is designed to address the requisite functions and to clarify other aspects of the NSC Staff that have been long neglected. Paragraph one outlines the Staff's responsibilities for the execution of the requisite functions and provides bureaucratic mechanisms by which these functions can be accomplished. Paragraph two provides a defined, vertical NSC Staff structure that allows for flexibility and accountability. Next, the directive caps the size of the Staff and requires that a cross-section of national security talent be employed. Paragraph four resolves a long-standing, if silent, element of friction within the government by identifying the equivalent rank for each position within the NSC Staff. Finally, the directive allows the APNSA some flexibility in the regional and functional groups but does not allow him to expand the size of the Staff or the scope of its responsibilities.

Such a document could be useful, not as a final product to be signed immediately by the president but as a vehicle to engender discussion long overdue and as a base upon which to construct a definitive articulation of the structure and functioning of the NSC Staff.

Conclusion

For the first 170 years of our country's existence, the management of its international affairs was quite effectively handled by the Department of State, with occasional help from the War and Navy Departments. With the end of the Second World War, however, the international environment began to change dramatically. Every administration since that of FDR has either moved to a White House–centered management structure or created a chaotic national security process. It is now time to formalize what has been the de facto system and create the sort of structure that will help guarantee the proper and efficient management of national security affairs into the next century. This can only be accomplished if we acknowledge the inability of an eighteenth-century system to deal with twenty-first century challenges and if we assign a formal, presidential mandate to the APNSA/NSA and the National Security Staff.

Conclusion

The Iran-Contra affair, if it accomplished nothing else, placed an institutional spotlight on the National Security Council Staff, subjecting it to scrutiny unprecedented in its forty-year history. It is important that we learn the right lessons from this experience and apply remedies that are appropriate to the problem. The most basic lesson is that the affair was symptomatic of a larger problem; it occurred not because the NSC Staff was too strong but rather because it was not designed to support the emerging realities of national security. The Iran-Contra affair is a manifestation of the much deeper issue that has plagued every administration since Truman—the structural-functional mismatch.

I am proposing remedies for this problem that are contrary to those proposed in many circles. They are based, in the first instance, on a recognition that the nature of contemporary national security and the challenges posed by the international and domestic environments demand that the president play the pivotal role in the national security system. It is no accident that every president since Kennedy has found the State Department wholly inadequate for the formulation of national security policy; indeed, the existence of foreign policy as a discipline separate from the broader sweep of national security is itself highly debatable. To paraphrase Clemenceau, diplomacy is now too important to be left to the diplomats.

The effective management of national security in the future will require a more thorough integration of the various components of national power—an integration that must take place in the White House. The seven functional requisites must form the foundation of this system. Imbedded in these functional requisites is the duality of the NSC Staff. The Staff must both serve the National Security Council as an institution and serve as the president's personal staff. Once this duality is recognized and accepted, the functional requisites flow as a natural consequence.

The national security system fashioned by any administration must support the execution of these requisite functions. Although forms, committee names, and specific responsibilities will vary, several principles should be followed:

1. The president must be at the center of the national security process. There can be no vicar for this position.
2. The APNSA and the NSC Staff must chair at least one of the key NSC subcommittees at each level of the national security structure.
3. The system must promote intellectual competition. Such competition becomes dysfunctional only when there are no institutionalized avenues for resolution.
4. The system must support the dual roles of the APNSA/NSA and the NSC Staff. The NSA and the Staff must have direct access to the president.
5. The system's design and the functional responsibilities of the Staff must be clearly directed by the president in a written document at the beginning of the administration. Changes must be similarly formalized.

If these principles are followed, the prospects for a reduced structural-functional mismatch and for an effective national security system are greatly improved. It is significant to note that the Bush administration adopted several of these principles in National Security Directive–1, in which the APNSA was given the chair of the Principals Committee and the deputy APNSA was to chair the Deputies Committee.[1]

It is important to make a final comment about people. Our discussion has focused extensively on systems, structure, and organization, but it is the people who actually make it all work. The most skillfully designed national security system will fail utterly when it is not staffed by men and women of great character, intellect, and commitment. More than any other organization in Washington, the NSC Staff depends upon its people. There are no insulating layers to screen the system from the egocentric, the foolish, and the venal. The president must, therefore, select his APNSA with the knowledge that it should be his most important—and careful—appointment. The APNSA must then select his Staff with equal care, demanding the highest standards of demonstrated competence, intellectual daring, and selfless dedication.

Driven by the demands of the national security system, the National Security Council Staff will continue to occupy a position of prominence into the next century. The president should take it as a task of the first order to design a system that recognizes the functional requisites and the central role that the president must exercise in the management of national security. The challenges of the twenty-first century demand no less.

Notes

Chapter 1

1. Throughout this discussion, several abbreviations will be used. The assistant to the president for national security affairs will appear as APNSA. Occasionally, this position will be referred to as the national security adviser (NSA). The NSC Staff will often be called the Staff.

2. This perspective is reflected in the composition of the original NSC; of its original seven members, four represented the defense community.

3. Cited by R. Gordon Hoxie, "About This Issue," in *Presidential Studies Quarterly* 17, no. 1 (Winter 1987), p. 13.

4. Alexander M. Haig, *Caveat: Realism, Reagan, and Foreign Policy* (New York: MacMillan Publishing Company, 1984), p. 58.

5. Ernest R. May, "The Development of Political-Military Consultation in the United States," in Karl F. Inderfurth and Loch K. Johnson, eds., *Decisions of the Highest Order* (Pacific Grove, Calif.: Brooks/Cole Publishing Company, 1988), p. 9.

6. Ibid., p. 10.

7. John E. Endicott, "The National Security Council: Formalized Coordination and Policy Planning," in Robert L. Pfaltzgraff, Jr., and Uri Ra'anan, *National Security Policy: The Decision-making Process* (Hamden, Conn.: Archon Books, 1984), p. 177.

8. May, pp. 11–12.

9. Ibid., p. 12.

10. Inderfurth and Johnson, p. 3.

11. Ibid.

12. Cited in John Tower, Edmund Muskie, and Brent Scowcroft, *Report of the President's Special Review Board* (Washington, D.C.: U.S. Government Printing Office, 1987), p. II-1.

13. "The National Security Act of 1947," in Inderfurth and Johnson, p. 38.

14. Ferdinand Eberstadt, "Post War Organization for National Security," in Inderfurth and Johnson, p. 33.

15. Tower et al., p. II-2.

16. Inderfurth and Johnson, p. 42.

17. Barry Rubin, *Secrets of State* (New York: Oxford University Press, 1985), p. 65.

18. Zbigniew Brzezinski, "The NSC's Midlife Crisis," in *Foreign Policy* 69 (Winter 87–88), p. 81.

19. John Allen Williams, "The National Security Establishment: Institutional Framework for Policymaking," in Stephen J. Cimbala, ed., *National Security Strategy: Choices and Limits* (New York: Praeger Publishers, 1984), p. 326.

20. Sidney W. Souers, "Policy Formulation for National Security," in Inderfurth and Johnson, p. 50.

21. Ibid., p. 54.

22. Cited in Inderfurth and Johnson, p. 43.

23. I. M. Destler, Leslie H. Gelb, and Anthony Lake, *Our Own Worst Enemy: The Unmaking of American Foreign Policy* (New York, Simon and Schuster, 1984), p. 171–172.

24. Cutler's role as the special assistant is often cited as the model by those who oppose an activist APNSA.

25. Robert Cutler, "The Development of the National Security Council," in Inderfurth and Johnson, p. 64.

26. Stanley L. Falk, "The NSC Under Truman and Eisenhower," in Inderfurth and Johnson, p. 75.

27. Tower et al., p. II-4.

28. "Organizing for National Security," in Inderfurth and Johnson, p. 84. This report of the Jackson Subcommittee has been described as the most comprehensive examination of the NSC system prior to the Tower Commission.

29. Henry J. Jackson, "Forging a Strategy for Survival," in Inderfurth and Johnson, p. 80.

30. Brzezinski, p. 86.

31. Endicott, p. 188.

32. McGeorge Bundy, "Letter to the Jackson Subcommittee," in Inderfurth and Johnson, p. 107.

33. Cited in Endicott, p. 188.

34. Williams, p. 327.

35. Henry Kissinger, *The White House Years* (Boston: Little, Brown, and Company, 1979), p. 42.

36. Ibid., p. 38.

37. Ibid., p. 39. For the record, it was at the beginning of the Nixon administration that the "Special" was dropped from the APNSA's title. Neither Kissinger nor Nixon knew what it meant.

38. Cited in Sam C. Sarkesian, "Presidential Leadership and National Security Policy," in Cimbala, p. 306.

Chapter 2

1. John Tower, Edmund Muskie, and Brent Scowcroft, *Report of the President's Special Review Board* (Washington, D.C.: U.S. Government Printing Office, 1987), p. I-3.

2. "The National Security Act of 1947," in Karl F. Inderfurth and Loch K. Johnson, eds., *Decisions of the Highest Order* (Pacific Grove, Calif.: Brooks/Cole Publishing Company, 1988), p. 38.

3. I. M. Destler, "A Job That Doesn't Work," in Inderfurth and Johnson, p. 324.

4. Philip A. Odeen, "The Role of the National Security Council," in Inderfurth and Johnson, p. 344.

5. Zbigniew Brzezinski, *Power and Principle* (New York: Farrar, Straus, and Giroux, 1983), p. 76.

6. Gary Sick, *All Fall Down* (New York: Random House, 1985), p. 209. Sick acknowledges that, upon Vance's return, he was afforded a special NSC meeting to review the bidding. This was, however, more to sooth Vance's wounded feelings than to reopen the debate; the president's mind was already made up.

7. Alexander M. Haig, *Caveat: Realism, Reagan, and Foreign Policy* (New York: MacMillan Publishing Company, 1984), p. 83.

8. "The National Security Act of 1947," in Inderfurth and Johnson, p. 38.

9. Destler, pp. 322–324; Leslie H. Gelb, "The Struggle Over Foreign Policy," in *The New York Times Magazine*, 20 July 1980, p. 35.

10. Brent Scowcroft, in Lawrence J. Korb and Keith D. Hahn, eds., *National Security Policy Organization in Perspective* (Washington, D.C.: American Enterprise Institute, 1981), p. 8. This is a transcript of a panel discussion held amongst Scowcroft, Philip Odeen, Leslie Gelb, Peter Szanton, William Hyland, David Aaron, John Kester, and Barry Blechman.

11. Tower et al., p. II-3.

12. Scowcroft, p. 30, argues that "I think the least of our worries is that we are going to overintegrate our system."

13. Stanley L. Falk, "The NSC Under Truman and Acheson," in Inderfurth and Johnson, p. 75.

14. Philip Odeen, in Korb and Hahn, p. 26.

15. Tower et al., p. V-5.

16. Zbigniew Brzezinski, "Deciding Who Makes Foreign Policy," in Inderfurth and Johnson, p. 327.

17. Acheson talks about the "anguish of decision" that is the first responsibility of a president. Dean Acheson, *Present at the Creation* (New York: Norton, 1969), p. 733.

18. Odeen, "The Role of the National Security Council," p. 344.

19. Scowcroft, p. 9.

20. Richard M. Nixon, *The Memoirs of Richard Nixon* (New York: Grosset and Dunlap, 1978), p. 927.

21. Cited in Barry Rubin, *Secrets of State* (New York: Oxford University Press, 1985), p. 99. This passage was part of a letter written by Rusk to incoming Secretary of State George Shultz in 1982.

22. For example, in late 1981, Ronald Reagan made a policy decision on how to handle Ethiopia's Marxist leader Mengistu. A State Department desk officer charged with managing U.S.-Ethiopian relations stated in an implementation meeting that the president did not understand the issue and that he was not going to follow the president's guidance. "After all," he said, "Ronald Reagan won't be here after 1984 and I will."

23. Tower et al., p. V-3.

24. Theodore C. Sorensen, "The President and the Secretary of State," in Inderfurth and Johnson, p. 336.

25. David Aaron, in Korb and Hahn, p. 32.

26. Constantine Menges, *Inside the National Security Council* (New York: Simon and Schuster, 1988), p. 358.

27. Tower et al., p. V-3.

28. Odeen, "The Role of the National Security Council," p. 366.

29. Robert C. McFarlane, Richard Saunders, and Thomas C. Shull, "The National Security Council: Organization for Policy Making," in R. Gordon Hoxie, ed., *The Presidency and National Security Policy* (New York: Center for the Study of the Presidency, 1984), p. 266.

30. Brzezinski, "The NSC's Midlife Crisis," in *Foreign Policy* 69 (Winter 87–88), p. 95.

31. Charles F. Hermann, "International Crises as a Situation Variable," in James N. Rosenau, ed., *International Politics and Foreign Policy* (New York: The Free Press, 1969), p. 414.

32. Odeen, in Korb and Hahn, p. 7.

33. Ibid.

34. Aaron, in Korb and Hahn, p. 14.

35. Ibid.

36. John Allen Williams, "The National Security Establishment: Institutional Framework for Policymaking," in Stephen J. Cimbala,

ed., *National Security Strategy: Choices and Limits* (New York: Praeger Publishers, 1984), p. 323.

37. Henry Kissinger, *The White House Years* (Boston: Little, Brown and Company, 1979), p. 30.

38. Brzezinski, "The NSC's Midlife Crisis," pp. 81–82.

39. Ibid., p. 92.

40. Cited in I. M. Deslter, Leslie H. Gelb, and Anthony Lake, *Our Own Worst Enemy: The Unmaking of American Foreign Policy* (New York: Simon and Schuster, 1984), p. 277.

41. Richard Brown, "Toward Coherence in Foreign Policy: Greater Presidential Control of the Foreign Policymaking Machinery," in Hoxie, pp. 326–327.

42. Cited in Inderfurth and Johnson, p. 91.

43. R. Gordon Hoxie, in *Presidential Studies Quarterly* (Winter 1987), p. 10.

44. Rubin, p. 116.

45. Kissinger, p. 11.

46. Rubin, pp. 132–142.

47. Scowcroft, p. 40.

48. Sam C. Sarkesian, "Presidential Leadership and National Security Policy," in Cimbala, p. 308.

49. Jimmy Carter, *Keeping Faith: Memoirs of a President* (New York: Bantam Books, 1982), p. 53.

50. Leslie Gelb, "Why Not the State Department?" in Charles W. Kegley and Eugene R. Wittkopf, *Perspectives in American Foreign Policy* (New York: St. Martin's Press, 1983), p. 286.

51. Ibid., p. 287.

52. Duncan L. Clarke, "Why State Can't Lead," in *Foreign Policy* 66 (Spring 1987), p. 135.

53. The Policy Planning Staff, established in 1949, is normally not manned by Foreign Service officers, placing it at a decided disadvantage. The single most important contribution for which the Policy Planning Staff is usually credited is the development of NSC-68 in 1950. Even in this, however, there is a dispute over whether NSC-68 would have had any relevance if the Korean War had not occurred.

54. Cited in Ernest R. May, "The Development of Political-Military Consultations in the United States," in Inderfurth and Johnson, p. 7.

55. Amos A. Jordan and William J. Taylor, *American National Security: Policy and Process* (Baltimore: The Johns Hopkins University Press, 1981), p. 202. This model, borrowed in turn from Roger Hilsman, has been modified by adding an additional layer and by emphasizing the bureaucratic dimension more strongly.

56. Scowcroft, p. 32.

57. Carnes Lord, *The Presidency and the Management of National Security* (New York: The Free Press, 1988), p. 89.

Chapter 3

1. Zbigniew Brzezinski, *Power and Principle* (New York: Farrar, Straus, Giroux, 1983), p. 8.

2. Ibid., p. 9.

3. I. M. Destler, Leslie H. Gelb, and Anthony Lake, *Our Own Worst Enemy: The Unmaking of American Foreign Policy* (New York: Simon and Schuster, 1984), p. 217.

4. William Hyland, in Lawrence J. Korb and Keith D. Hahn, eds., *National Security Policy Organization in Perspective* (Washington, D.C.: American Enterprise Institute, 1981), p. 38.

5. Jimmy Carter, *Presidential Directive/NSC-2, The National Security Council System* (Washington, D.C.: The White House, 1977), p. 1. Hereafter, this document will be called PD-2.

6. Henry Kissinger, *The White House Years* (Boston: Little, Brown and Company, 1979), p. 38.

7. Brzezinski, p. 59.

8. PD-2 says that the membership of the PRC shall consist of "the statutory members of the NSC and the Assistant for National Security Affairs," implying that the president and the vice president are included. This was never done and was obviously never intended.

9. Carter, *PD-2*, p. 2.

10. Brzezinski, p. 59. He says "the PRC met most often under the chairmanship of the Secretary of State, occasionally under the Secretary of Defense, and only two or three times under the Secretary of the Treasury."

11. Carter, *PD-2*, p. 3.

12. The distinction is subtle; of the seven important subcommittees in the Nixon administration, Kissinger chaired six of them, but they were not formally constituted, cabinet-level organizations.

13. Brzezinski, p. 60.

14. Destler et al., p. 223.

15. Brzezinski, p. 66.

16. Ibid., p. 61.

17. Cyrus Vance, *Hard Choices* (New York: Simon and Schuster, 1983), p. 37. There was a nominal effort to change this system when

Muskie replaced Vance as secretary of state, but nothing really came of it.

18. At the mini-SCC, attended by David McGiffert (ASD-ISA) and David Newsom (under secretary of state-PA), with David Aaron in the chair, it was decided to forego the exercise in order to avoid a confrontation with Qaddafhi.

19. Brzezinski, p. 177.

20. Ibid., pp. 51–52.

21. The difficulties in the PRM process are evidenced by the unresponsiveness of the system to a request for a PRM on the Persian Gulf in the aftermath of the collapse of the Shah of Iran. Most people agreed with the need for such a study, but nobody wanted to undertake the bureaucratic wrestling match to get one under way.

22. Cited in Destler et al., p. 225.

23. In his memoirs, Haig talks repeatedly about NSDD-1. In fact, NSDD-1 was an innocuous document defining the terms of national security. His proposal would have become NSDD-2.

24. Ed Meese's briefcase became something of a punchline in the early Reagan years. If an idea or a proposal went "into Meese's briefcase," it had been rejected, discarded, or more likely, not understood.

25. Ronald Reagan, *National Security Decision Directive Number 2: National Security Council Structure* (Washington, D.C.: The White House, 1982), p. 1. This document will hereafter be called NSDD-2.

26. Alexander M. Haig, *Caveat: Realism, Reagan, and Foreign Policy* (New York: MacMillan Publishing Company, 1984), p. 85.

27. Zbigniew Brzezinski, "The NSC's Midlife Crisis," in *Foreign Policy* 69 (Winter 87–88), p. 89.

28. Allen was investigated for allegations that he had accepted $1,000 from some Japanese reporters for arranging an interview with Nancy Reagan. He was subsequently cleared of any wrongdoing. Somewhat ironically, the $1,000 was initially discovered in a safe that was being cleared out for some temporary occupants to use during the AWACS debate in 1981. Among these temporary occupants who found the money was Oliver North.

29. Donald T. Regan, *For the Record: From Wall Street to Washington* (New York: Harcourt, Brace, Jovanovich, Publishers, 1988), p. 55.

30. Haig, p. 74.

31. The tremendous frustration of the Staff members in this role cannot be overstated.

32. Interview with Lieutenant General (Ret.) William E. Odom, 20 January 1989.

33. Brzezinski, "The NSC's Midlife Crisis," p. 90.

34. Sam C. Sarkesian, "Presidential Leadership and National Security Policy," in Stephen J. Cimbala, ed., *National Security Strategy: Choices and Limits* (New York: Praeger Publishers, 1984), p. 312.

35. Karl F. Inderfurth and Loch K. Johnson, eds., *Decisions of the Highest Order* (Pacific Grove, Calif.: Brooks/Cole Publishing Company, 1988), p. 195.

36. Cited in Harrison Donnelly, "National Security Council," in *Editorial Research Reports*, vol. 1, no. 2 (January 16, 1987), p. 26.

37. Cited in Donnelly, pp. 19–20.

38. Philip Odeen, "The Role of the National Security Council," in Inderfurth and Johnson, p. 344.

39. Coordination is often in the eyes of the beholder. Brzezinski, Brown, and Aaron all contend that the process worked well and that, as the issues became more clearly defined, certain agencies were dropped from the coordination process. Others, such as Muskie and Gelb, argue that Brzezinski dropped the State Department from the coordinating process prematurely because the department had some significant reservations about the issue.

40. The ERW debacle stemmed from the reversal of President Carter's decision to produce and deploy the warheads in Europe. After European leaders, most notably Helmut Schmidt, had spent some political capital in paving the way for the controversial deployments, Carter unilaterally reversed his position, causing great consternation in the Alliance.

41. Reagan, *NSDD-2*, p. 1.

42. Cited in Donnelly, p. 22.

43. Tower et al., p. B-3.

44. Carter, *PD-2*, p. 3.

45. Reagan, *NSDD-2*, p. 1.

46. Carter, *Keeping Faith: Memoirs of a President* (New York: Bantam Books, 1982), p. 53.

47. Interview with Zbigniew Brzezinski, 15 January 1981.

48. Brzezinski, *Power and Principle*, p. 468.

49. Haig, p. 86.

50. Brzezinski, *Power and Principle*, p. 477.

51. Warren Christopher, "The Iran Hostage Crisis, 1980," in Inderfurth and Johnson, p. 207.

52. Destler et al., p. 223.

53. Reagan, *NSDD-2*, p. 7.

54. One of the reasons that NSDD-2 does not address crisis management is that it was issued some nine months after NSDD-3,

the crisis management document. It would have been somewhat embarrassing to reference NSDD-3 in a document that should have been issued a full year before it was actually promulgated.

55. Vance argued that crisis management "was properly the responsibility of the Secretary of State." Brzezinski, *Power and Principle,* p. 62.

56. The term "special situation" was used for two reasons. First, the drafters felt that the group should be able to convene without alarming an ever-attentive media. Second, the drafters felt that the more general term would allow the group to address a wider range of issues than those normally subsumed under the heading of crises.

57. Constantine Menges, *Inside the National Security Council* (New York: Simon and Schuster, 1988), pp. 68–70, 74, 76, 82.

58. Robert C. McFarlane, Richard Saunders, and Thomas C. Shull, "The National Security Council: Organization for Policy Making," in R. Gordon Hoxie, ed., *The Presidency and National Security Policy* (New York: Center for the Study of the Presidency, 1984), p. 271.

59. Carter, *Keeping Faith: Memoirs of a President,* p. 53.

60. McFarlane, for example, stated that the "NSA must occasionally be a policy initiator," clearly indicating the secondary nature of that function. McFarlane et al., p. 266.

61. Ibid., p. 262.

62. The first NSSD to be issued was on global strategy. It was entitled NSSD 1-82, rather than NSSD-1, because the drafters felt that it would be embarrassing to admit, through the numbering system, that this was the first NSSD issued by an administration a full year old. By adding the year, it was felt that this would camouflage the problem.

63. Odeen, p. 345.

64. Interview with Dr. Richard Pipes, 23 January 1989.

65. Tower et al., p. I-3.

Chapter 4

1. The secretary of the treasury and other members of the government were not added as formal members of the NSC; they became regularly invited participants, but the legislation itself was not changed. During the Reagan administration, so many ad hoc members were added that NSC meetings became unwieldy. As a result, the National Security Planning Group (NSPG) was instituted to shrink the size back to manageable proportions.

2. In the beginning of the Bush administration, the attendees of NSC meetings were reduced in number, reverting back to the actual statutory members.

3. Dimitri K. Simes, "If the Cold War Is Over, Then What?" in *The New York Times*, 27 December 1988, p. A21.

4. Karen Elliott House, "The 90s and Beyond," in *The Wall Street Journal*, 23 January 1989, p. A1.

5. R. Jeffrey Smith, "Arms Cuts Gain Favor as Tensions Ease," in *The Washington Post*, 8 May 1989.

6. Andrew J. Goodpaster, *Gorbachev and the Future of East-West Security: A Report for the Mid-Term* (Washington, D.C.: The Atlantic Council, April 1989), p. 7. In the same occasional paper, Goodpaster argued for a significant reduction in U.S. forces deployed in Europe in conjunction with similar Soviet cuts.

7. For a theoretical discussion of the flow of influence between the superpowers and the Third World, see Christopher C. Shoemaker and John Spanier, *Patron-Client State Relationships* (New York: Praeger, 1984).

8. Dimitri K. Simes, "Even if Gorbachev Falls, Detente Will Last," in *The New York Times*, 20 March 1989, p. A19.

9. Zbigniew Brzezinski, "A Proposition the Soviets Shouldn't Refuse?" in *The New York Times*, 13 March 1989, p. A19.

10. Michael I. Handel, "The Future of Dominant-Subordinate Systems," in Jan F. Triska, ed., *Dominant Powers and Subordinate States* (Durham: Duke University Press, 1986), p. 439.

11. Caspar W. Weinberger, "The Uses of Military Power," in *Defense 88* (January 1985), pp. 7–9.

12. Richard Nixon, "American Foreign Policy: The Bush Agenda," in *Foreign Affairs: America and the World*, vol. 68, no. 1 (1988/1989), p. 205.

13. Robert Kaiser, "The U.S.S.R. in Decline," in *Foreign Affairs 67*, no. 2 (Winter 1988/1989), p. 97.

14. Nixon, p. 202.

15. Paul Quinn-Judge, "Military Faces a New Foe: Criticism," in *The Christian Science Monitor*, 3 February 1989, p. 3.

16. Zbigniew Brzezinski, "Will the Soviet Empire Self-Destruct?" in *The New York Times Magazine*, 26 February 1989, p. 38.

17. The Soviet Union constructed a phased-array radar at Krasnoyarsk in the middle of the Soviet Union during the late 1970s and early 1980s, in violation of the ABM Treaty. The United States discovered this and created a major furor over the issue of cheating, much to the dismay of Gorbachev, who indirectly ascribed the violation

to an overzealous military. The facility never actually became operational.

18. Ronald Reagan, *The National Security Strategy of the United States* (Washington, D.C.: U.S. Government Printing Office, 1988), p. 35.

19. Handel, p. 439.

20. Don Oberdorfer, "Eased East-West Tensions Offer Possibilities, Risks," in *The Washington Post*, 7 May 1989, p. A1.

21. David Gergen, "Can We Have an Effective Presidency?" in *Presidential Studies Quarterly* 18, no. 3 (Summer 1988), p. 483.

22. Paul Kennedy, *The Rise and Fall of the Great Powers* (New York: Random House, 1987); Samuel P. Huntington, "The U.S.—Decline or Renewal," in *Foreign Affairs* 67, no. 2 (Winter 1988/1989), pp. 76–96; Charles A. Kupchan, "Empire, Military Power, and Economic Decline," in *International Security* 13, no. 4 (Spring 1989), pp. 36–53.

23. C. Michael Aho and Marc Levinson, "The Economy After Reagan," in *Foreign Affairs* 67, no. 2 (Winter 1988/1989), p. 21.

24. Robert J. McCartney, "Europe Seeks an Economy of Scale," in *The Washington Post*, 19 March 1989, p. A1.

25. Ibid.

26. Philip Revzin, "Europeans Begin Planning for the Day When US Troops Go Home," in *The Wall Street Journal*, 17 February 1989, p. A10.

27. Edward N. Luttwak, "The Alliance Without an Enemy," in *The New York Times*, 3 February 1989, p. A31.

28. Reagan, p. 25.

29. For a discussion of the sad history of PD-13 and security assistance, see Andrew K. Semmel, "Evolving Patterns of US Security Assistance, 1950–1980," in Charles W. Kegley and Eugene R. Wittkopf, *Perspectives on American Foreign Policy* (New York: St. Martin's Press, 1983).

30. Gerald F. Seib, "US Public Shift in National Security Poses Problems for US Policy Makers," in *The Wall Street Journal*, 17 October 1988, p. A18.

31. Jessica Tuchman Matthews, "Redefining Security," in *Foreign Affairs* 68, no. 2 (Spring 1989), p. 162.

32. William J. Broad, "Soviet Photos of US Were for Spying," in *The New York Times*, 30 January 1989, p. A2.

33. Walt B. Wriston, "Technology and Sovereignty," in *Foreign Affairs* 67, no. 2 (Winter 1988/1989), p. 69.

34. Nixon, p. 210.

35. Matthews, p. 162.

36. This effort was part of Brzezinski's Persian Gulf Security Framework, a far-reaching program to construct a comprehensive strategy for securing vital U.S. interests in the Gulf region. This, in turn, was an integral part of the effort to put substance behind the Carter Doctrine announced in 1980.

37. Paul F. Gorman, *Commitment to Freedom* (Washington, D.C.: The Pentagon, 1988). This was one of the studies that supported the Ikle-Wohlstetter Commission and its product, *Discriminant Deterrence* (Washington, D.C.: U.S. Government Printing Office, 1988). *Discriminant Deterrence* represented the views of many of the most distinguished students of national security and had important operational implications. Unfortunately, it was presented in the last year of the Reagan administration and, therefore, had no real impact on national security strategy.

38. Nick Kotz, *Wild Blue Yonder* (Princeton: Princeton University Press, 1988), p. 8.

39. Frank C. Carlucci, *Annual Report to the Congress* (Washington, D.C.: U.S. Government Printing Office, 1989, p. 119).

40. Kotz, p. 96.

41. Ibid., p. 238.

42. Carlucci, p. 119.

43. Lee H. Hamilton, "Congress and the Presidency in American Foreign Policy," in *Presidential Studies Quarterly* 18, no. 3 (Summer 1988), p. 507. Hamilton, as a long-standing member of the House of Representatives, lends a special degree of credibility to these assertions.

44. Zbigniew Brzezinski, *In Quest of National Security* (Boulder: Westview Press, 1988), p. 71.

45. John T. Rourke and Russell Farnen, "War, Presidents, and the Constitution," in *Presidential Studies Quarterly* 18, no. 3 (Summer 1988), p. 513.

46. Hamilton, p. 508.

47. Ibid., p. 509.

48. Gergen, p. 477.

49. Kotz, p. 240.

50. Brzeżinski, *In Quest of National Security*, p. 78.

51. Ibid.

52. Rourke and Farnen, pp. 518–519.

53. Reagan, p. 15.

54. Carlucci, p. 74.

55. Admittedly, some in the government, such as Richard Perle, sought clear-cut U.S. superiority, feeling that this was the best way

to insure stability and implicitly rejecting the doctrine of Mutually Assured Destruction.

56. Strobe Talbott, *Deadly Gambits* (New York: Alfred A. Knopf, 1984), pp. 260–262, talks about this unusual alliance. The Department of State's support, led by Richard Burt, was not primarily due to the Department's sympathy with the JCS SIOP concerns but rather was due to Burt's feeling that this was the approach that had the best chance of forming the basis for a START agreement.

57. Daniel Charles, *Nuclear Planning in NATO* (Cambridge, Mass.: Ballinger Publishing Company, 1987), p. 124.

58. During the 1986 summit at Reykjavik, there was serious talk between President Reagan and General Secretary Gorbachev about an agreement to ban all ICBMs from both sides, a proposal that had not been presented to the allies first and raised a feal firestorm of doubt about the strength of the U.S. commitment to European security. Fortunately for all concerned, this proposal was allowed to die with little serious subsequent consideration.

59. In May 1989, President Bush proposed a 10 percent cut in the U.S. military presence in Europe if the Soviets would agree to cut their forces to levels equal to those of the United States. This proposal did much to heal the highly publicized split in the alliance over the success of the Gorbachev initiatives and the speed with which the United States would enter into negotiations with the Soviet Union on short-range nuclear forces in Europe.

60. Talbott, p. 345.

61. Carnes Lord, *The Presidency and the Management of National Security* (New York: The Free Press, 1988), p. 3.

Chapter 5

1. John Tower, Edmund Muskie, and Brent Scowcroft, *Report of the President's Special Review Board* (Washington, D.C.: U.S. Government Printing Office, 1987), p. I-3.

2. Leslie Gelb, in Lawrence J. Korb and Keith D. Hahn, eds., *National Security Policy Organization in Perspective* (Washington, D.C.: American Enterprise Institute, 1981), p. 19.

3. Philip Odeen, in Korb and Hahn, p. 24.

4. Tower et al., p. V-2.

5. Odeen, p. 9.

6. Tower et al., p. V-3.

7. Harold Brown, *Thinking About National Security* (Boulder: Westview Press, 1983), p. 202.

8. Alexander M. Haig, *Caveat: Realism, Reagan, and Foreign Policy* (New York: MacMillan Publishing Company, 1984), p. 58.

9. I. M. Destler, "The Job That Doesn't Work," in Karl F. Inderfurth and Loch K. Johnson, *Decisions of the Highest Order* (Pacific Grove, Calif.: Brooks/Cole Publishing Company, 1988), pp. 320–324.

10. Ibid., p. 322.

11. Inderfurth and Johnson, p. 296.

12. Zbigniew Brzezinski, "Deciding Who Makes Foreign Policy," in Inderfurth and Johnson, pp. 328–329; R. D. McLaurin, "National Security Policy: New Problems and Proposals," in R. Gordon Hoxie, *The Presidency and National Security Policy* (New York: Center for the Study of the Presidency, 1984), p. 350.

13. Haig, p. 60.

14. Carnes Lord, *The Presidency and the Management of National Security* (New York: The Free Press, 1988), p. 119.

15. Harrison Donnelly, *The National Security Council* (Washington, D.C.: Congressional Quarterly's Editorial Research Reports, 16 January 1987), p. 22.

16. Lord, p. 120.

17. Brent Scowcroft, in Korb and Hahn, p. 8.

18. The Scowcroft NSC staff in the Bush administration began at numbers lower than those of the Reagan administration.

19. Tower et al., p. V-4.

20. McGeorge Bundy, "Letter to Jackson Subcommittee," in Inderfurth and Johnson, p. 107.

21. Tower et al., p. V-4.

22. Jimmy Carter, *Presidential Directive/NSC-2: The National Security Council System* (Washington, D.C.: The White House, 1977), p. 2.

Conclusion

1. Leslie H. Gelb, "Who Makes Foreign Policy?" in *The New York Times*, 3 February 1989, p. A30; David Hoffman, "Bush Scales Back Security Council," in *The Washington Post*, 3 February 1989, p. A8.

About the Book and Author

Since its creation in 1947, the NSC has played an increasingly important role in the formation of U.S. national security policy. Christopher C. Shoemaker, a former staff member of the NSC, describes the history, functioning, and weaknesses of the NSC and its staff system and suggests changes that could improve the NSC's performance. This work will be of interest to anyone concerned about U.S. foreign policy and the contemporary structure of American government.

Christopher C. Shoemaker is a professional military officer who served on the staff of the NSC during both the Carter and Reagan administrations. He received his Ph.D. in political science from the University of Florida in 1981, and he is coauthor, with John Spanier, of *Patron-Client State Relationships.*

Index